Shri Parthasarathi Rajagopalachariji
President
Shri Ram Chandra Mission

What is Sahaj Marg

Revised Edition

What is Sahaj Marg

Revised Edition

Lectures and Discussions from the Preceptors' Seminars on Sahaj Marg

July 10 - September 28, 1988
in West Point, USA and Courmettes, France

by

Shri Parthasarathi Rajagopalachari

First Edition:1988, 1000 Copies (For Preceptors Only)
Second Edition:1994, 2000 Copies (Revised Edition)

This book has been previously published by Shri Ram Chandra Mission, India under the title of *What is Sahaj Marg? (A Preceptor's Guide)*.

All rights reserved

©Shri Ram Chandra Mission
North American Publishing Committee
Molena, GA, USA, 1994

No part of this book may be reproduced in any form or by any means without permission in writing from Shri Ram Chandra Mission.

Printed in USA

ISBN 0-945242-26-3

Contents

I Lectures
1 Education — Means and Purpose..................3
2 The Master, the Mission, and the Method..................13
3 The Role of the Master..................39
4 Stages of Spiritual Progress..................71
5 Stages of Spiritual Evolution..................97
6 Faith..................133

II Questions and Answers
7 Sunday, July 10, 1988..................147
8 Tuesday, July 12, 1988..................153
9 Wednesday, July 13, 1988..................171
10 Thursday, July 14, 1988..................193
11 Friday, July 15, 1988..................223

Samarth Guru Mahatma Ram Chandraji Maharaj
of
Fatehgarh (U.P.)

Shri Ram Chandraji
of
Shahjahanpur (U.P.)
Founder-President
Shri Ram Chandra Mission

I

Lectures

1

Education — Means and Purpose

West Point, USA
Monday, September 26, 1988

Dear brothers and sisters,

I had an experimental seminar in France, I think it was the third week of July, or the second week of July. It was the mid-week of the thirteen weeks seminar, six before and six after, and this was the one week. Everybody knew about it well in advance. They had a lot of time to prepare themselves, to think about it. Yet, when they came to the seminar, I think we were about a hundred and thirty preceptors all together there, I could feel a good deal of resentment, considerable suspicion, a fair bit of anger, and in some preceptors a lot of resistance to the idea of that seminar. I could feel it. It was there, very palpable in the air. But of course, I was prepared for it. Anything new is always subject to resistance; that is a part of the human makeup. So I was not at all surprised, though I was a little surprised at the degree of that resistance, the scope of that resistance. Some could not care less. They came, but as very angry individuals.

Anyway we started off the first day and I gave the practical work on the first day itself. Of course that created a turmoil, because they all thought they were going to listen to a nice talk, or perhaps not so nice. But yet a talk is a talk, you know, you can listen to it and, in the good old biblical tradition, take it through one ear and throw it out through the other, and go back home happy. But when I gave them the practical work I think nearly everybody was upset. Now that is not very surprising

West Point

because when you think of adult literacy in countries like India and other backward nations, where adults have to be educated, it is very difficult to get them into schools. Because there is this crazy idea, you know, and the West is no less crazy than the East in this idea, that education is for the young. It is as if education starts at the age of three, three and a half, in the kindergarten, and ends with a college degree at, I do not know, twenty-eight years of age here; it is twenty-one or twenty-two in India. In India if you talk to a man about education after he has graduated from school he will probably slap you. They think, "That is enough," you see, "That is education. I am now educated."

So the most important thing to get across is that education never stops. Learning may stop, you see, but education does not stop. Now we have to carefully distinguish between learning and education. We learn in schools, but education is a life-long process. We educate ourselves, people educate us, events educate us, the environment educates us. So the first crude understanding of education that we all have, that education should be confined to schools, is what you have to remove from your minds before you can be open to any system of education like ours. Education never ends. And it is wisdom to accept that one is not as educated as one thought, though one may have many degrees after one's name. And that aspect of the educational process must be understood: that it is like breathing which never stops as long as we are alive. It is like eating and drinking which do not stop as long as we are alive. Education too is a process, you see, which is co-existent with life.

So this, what shall I say, antagonism during the Courmettes seminar was quite a surprise only in its scope, though I was perfectly prepared for it, because I had been preparing for it for months ahead. Now, I gave them this first practical work

Education — Means and Purpose

session and all that was missing was screams. But it was there inside, you see, I could see it in their faces. I could see it in their gestures. I could see it in the way they looked at me, the way they stalked off with a hurt look on their faces. "You are testing me," you know, that sort of look. Anyway, I am happy to say they obeyed, you see, and went through the process on the first day. And then that evening they all brought their papers, which I refused to see. I said, "Sorry, it is not my intention to examine you like a child. This is a process. It is not for me to judge whether you are right or wrong. It is not that intention with which I have called you here and with which I gave you the test. It is for you to find out how well you know this job. So I will not look into your papers at all. But I would like to help you in this process of self-education by giving my own reading of the condition of these six or ten people I have given you as a panel for your study. And each one of you is welcome to compare your reading with mine and evaluate yourself." The relief was again almost palpable, visible.

Now this is a lesson to the educational systems of the world, that if you cannot educate a person without permitting the person under that process to retain his or her self-respect, the system will fail. You can see this in the success of the American educational system where students and teachers interact almost as if they are friends. I have seen sometimes the professor sitting like a student and the student sitting like the professor, behind the desk with his feet up on the table, "Hi, Prof." And I am surprised to see that in this arrogant West these professors are able to tolerate this nonsense from the students. In India they would get a beating. But that is the success of the educational system here — that by treating the student as a friend, allowing him to put his feet up on the chair, with his Reeboks or whatever, muddying it perhaps, you are able to get his confidence. You see, why I am saying this is education is

West Point

a process of evoking knowledge from you, not giving you knowledge. So when we are able to interact with that confidence and mutual trust, where the student can walk into the office and say, "Hey Frank, how about telling me how this darn thing works out." And he says, "Well, come along, let's look at it." And then you lead him step by step, not to an answer, but enable him to think for himself. "Oh, heck, I did not think of that," he says. Now he has learned permanently.

So teaching is a process where you help the other person to learn. You do not teach him anything except how to learn. I would request all of you to remember this because you all are preceptors, and you have to teach abhyasis. And the heavy-handed, dictatorial approach to education never works. It only produces resistance, resistors, and eventually disrupts the system.

After that there was a sense of satisfaction, calmness, a sense of over-all relief, you see, that this guy is not out to break us. He is only giving us an opportunity to learn. "Look at him, he does not even want to see our papers. That is great!" Then matters went a little more smoothly and, day after day, it was a bigger relief. Because I started off giving them a panel of ten persons whom they had to evaluate; next day I made it a little tougher by giving them a mix of advanced disciples, abhyasis, and not so advanced, and some beginners. They had no way of knowing. Next day I made them take preceptors. And then I think one day I said, "Pick out any one you want and give me a reading, even non-abhyasis." And I think the fifth day I said, "Pick out from a magazine or a newspaper any figure that appeals to you and give me a reading of that person." Some people even chose the Pope. And the sixth day was, of course, the final test. I said, "I would like you to give me a reading of myself." Now that reinforced their confidence.

Education — Means and Purpose

The way the problem was approached, the educational scheme was outlined, the graded approach to the whole affair, and finally making myself a subject of their, shall we say, experiment, and all in a very anonymous setting where I never saw the result, contributed to the seminar's effectiveness. You could see, you know, some people beaming with satisfaction. Obviously, when I gave them the reading and their's had tallied, their self-esteem, more than anything else, more than even their confidence, their esteem was reinforced, you see, "I have done it." And when the seminar ended, it was only, you know, out of the hundred and thirty people, barely a handful of persons, six or seven people, who never really made it, because they had no confidence. They never had faith in themselves. They started off with the idea they could not do it, and they never did anything. They did not work!

Why I am saying this is, at the end of the week, it was very obvious that the failures were not those who had attempted to do something and failed, but those who never attempted to do anything, and therefore were failures. They were not really failures, they were non-attemptees. This only goes to prove that those who attempt must succeed. If out of a hundred and thirty odd preceptors only six could not do anything, and out of the hundred and twenty-four, almost a hundred and twenty had, well, results in excess of eighty percent of success, it goes to show that native talent lies buried within all of us. We are all able to do it. And as Babuji said, "If you start off with the idea that you cannot do it, you will never be able to do it, even if God is inside you." Because it sort of punctures the will, you know. And where the will is lacking, nothing can be achieved. And then the most amusing part of this whole seminar was, I had a unanimous, I will not even say it was a request, it was not as polite as that, it was a demand, you see, that next year it should be at least two weeks, I mean, the preceptors' seminar.

West Point

You see the drama of the situation, starting off with near-total resistance, anger, annoyance, visibly written on everyone's face. I do not think there was an exception, perhaps only a few. And at the end of the week everyone was happy, everyone was satisfied, and everyone was telling me, "Chari, it is not at all difficult, you know, this reading business," as if I had told them it was difficult! And then clamouring for two weeks next year. Why I am giving you this background is that you should start off in an atmosphere of confidence that you are all capable individuals. The Master would not have chosen you otherwise. You were capable, your capacity was brought up to the level that was necessary to perform the task given to you, the service to humanity.

So let us not have faith in ourselves but let us have faith in that old man's choice of us. That he did not pick duds, you see, he always picked winners. When we lose faith in ourselves and sit down and put our heads into our palms and weep in frustration, more than anything else it shows lack of faith in that old man, the Master. And that is a very sad thing, you see, that we should not have faith in the Master who picked us.

So ultimately, you see, when you have confidence in this work, it is not self-confidence that we require, it is confidence in the Master that we require. It is confidence in the powers of the Master, his wisdom, his grace, his mercy, his charity, his ability to raise humanity out of this world into the other world. And when we are able to do that and sit in the thought that he is working, his powers are working, his grace is descending, his mercy is flowing, his love is enveloping, then you find that He is there. Then becomes possible this miracle of the self-transformation process, that at least for the nonce, at least for the moment, we are not there, the Master is there, and his work is perfect.

Education — Means and Purpose

There is no use in saying, you know, "Imagine that you are not there but the Master is sitting in your place. If necessary think his beard is there on your face." Yes, that is as a start, you see, to help you come into that state of being, that the Master is there, not you. But if it remains an artifice and every time you have to feel your face to see if the beard is there and you do not find it and you say, "Heck, I am not even able to make that guy come here," you have started off on the wrong foot, as it were. This is not a system of supposition where you sit down and try to feel the beard on your face. I mean, no girl preceptor is ever going to find a beard on her face. And most men do not either. Because it is not the beard which matters, it is the beard as an aid to bring him here, you see, in your mental supposition, which must work to effectively place him there. And when you are able to do that, you find now who is working — he is working. So what are we weeping about?

You see, this is the sense of confidence that I would like this process to instil in you. This is the approach with which I wish you all to start work today. I am not going to talk any more, this is the only talk I shall be giving during this three day seminar for you all. I would request you to listen to the tapes of the talks I gave in Courmettes first. There it was six days, here it has to be condensed to three days. The timing of it I leave to you to work out. It is two hours of business every day. Because approximately an hour each day for six days, six hours, so you may have to listen to two hours of those talks every morning, or one hour in the morning, one hour in the afternoon. And, in between, I think you should take two hours off to do some reading, practical reading. And you are free to choose today a panel of ten abhyasis for your work. Not each one a different ten, but ten with whom you will all work, one after the other. And put your readings down on paper, please, and keep it. Tomorrow you will have six preceptors from

West Point

among yourselves whom I shall nominate. Put a little salt and pepper into the thing. [laughter] [he chuckles] And that will be tomorrow's. The third day you can either take a random choice, you know, your cousin if you have her photograph or the Pope again, I have no objection. He is a silent partner in this training program; or Babuji, or me, anyone you like. And if you do this with this idea that, "Master is sitting there, I am not there," surely you do not have to think of this thing again. The training is finished.

So the whole process must start with the self, with the lower case 's', and end with the Self, with the upper case 'S'. That is all there is to it. On the computer it is a single jab of one finger. [he chuckles] And here it is not even that. You do not have to jab a finger, there is no 'control-Y', there is no delete. All that you have to do is in your mind. Lower case 's' gone, upper case 'S' here — He is there. As Babuji said, "Think of Him and He is there." So this is the small exercise, sisters and brothers, that I would like you to accept and undergo, and choose your times, choose the people, on this basis for the three days. Put it all down in writing, do not show it to me, tell me whom you have selected. I will give you my reading on a piece of paper. You are welcome to compare it. And you will find that you will come out with flying colors because you went in and He came out.

You see, that is the secret of the transformational process. In the ancient literature of the yogic tradition it is said that when you take a bath in a river, and if that bath has lasted twenty minutes, you come out a different person altogether, because most of the cells in your body have changed in that time. So if a mere dip in a river can change the physical human being and bring out a new human being, why cannot we enter the portals of the Master's temple and come out as Him? Here there is no question of my being changed into something which is still me.

Education — Means and Purpose

Every abhyasi must walk in as himself, and a Master must walk out. That is our responsibility to ourselves, that is our goal, and it is also our duty to the abhyasis who come to us. Frank must come in and Master must go out. Debbie must come in and Master must go out. Bill must come in and another Master must go out. It is like a factory, you take in so many raw materials but the product is the same which comes out. If the raw material went in at one end and came out as the raw material at the other end, what would you think of that factory? Or of those machines? So how can we accept here, you see, the truth, or the fact, that Bill went in and Bill came out?

So we are involved in a production process, which is a transformation process, where he who goes in never comes out again. Not because he has ceased to exist, or is dead, but because he has become transformed into the Master. I thank you all for your co-operation.

Thank you.

2

The Master, the Mission, and the Method

Courmettes, France
Sunday, July 10, 1988

Of course, it goes without saying we need your co-operation, Babuji always emphasized the need for co-operation whether we are abhyasis or preceptors or anything else, and he used to explain that co-operation is the first step towards the eventual step of surrender. And his one unfailing and often repeated advice: "How to create co-operation? Take interest!" You see, last night I was unable to sleep much so I had a thought, which might appeal to businessmen. In business, you put out capital to earn interest, here you take interest to build your capital. A principle of invertendo all over again.

So, the first principle of Sahaj Marg — take interest! As an abhyasi, take interest in your sadhana, in your evolution, in your ability to reach the goal. As a preceptor, take interest in the work that you have voluntarily undertaken. I do not think it has ever been thrusted on anybody who was not willing to take it up. On the contrary it has been difficult to, sort of, dissuade aspirants to preceptorship from aspiring to it. I have always said, even to my Master, that had I had the choice, I would never have been a preceptor. Because only when you get into it, and if you are conscientious about your work, if you are sincere to yourself, sincere to the Master, sincere to the abhyasis who come with so much longing in their hearts, demands, cravings, aspirations, then you will know it is perhaps a million times more difficult than a priest's job or a doctor's work. You see, in our society we are always praising the doctor and the priest. One as the doctor of the body, the other as the doctor of the soul. Unfortunately, today we are faced with a society where the moral degradation of these professions, because even priestcraft has become a profession today, where the moral degradation is almost complete. They are taking interest, but in themselves.

So please understand clearly what my Master, Ram Chandraji Maharaj, Babuji Maharaj, said, "Take interest not in yourself but in your work, in your responsibilities, in your evolution." Because when I take interest in myself, as I am today, it is selfish. And I, by that very act of taking interest in myself, put a bar to my advancement, because the interest is in myself, as I am, and I will continue to be what I am. Therefore, my evolution is stopped. This is perhaps one reason why selfishness obstructs all growth. But interest in the work, interest in the Master, interest in the Mission, interest in the abhyasis' welfare, it takes away our interest or self-centredness and projects it outside ourselves. And it makes for sincerity, for ability, for ultimately the Ultimate capacity.

So the first need — whether we are abhyasis or preceptors, and please remember we are both — for ourselves: we are abhyasis, each one of us has to grow. And you know, in Sahaj Marg the goal is infinite. Towards infinity is the way. The goal is ever beyond. Ever in sight but ever beyond. So, the need for not fixing ourselves at one position, or in one condition, or in one state of being, and saying, "Today I have reached my destination in Sahaj Marg," such a statement would be impossible. Even by the Master of Masters. Sahaj Marg knows no static condition. Sahaj Marg has no fixed situation. It is an ever-moving, ever-growing, ever-expanding, not only concept, but a possibility and an actuality, as proved for us in the lives of our two great Masters, Lalaji Maharaj and Babuji Maharaj.

The Master, the Mission, and the Method

So there is no room, ever, for satisfaction. Babuji always said, "If you are satisfied, there stops your progress." And I do not see why this concept of an ever-expanding, ever-receding goal should prove either difficult to understand, or frustrating in our experience, because science teaches us that the universe itself is ever-expanding. We are not in a static universe. And if the physical universe, which we are so much in love with, which appears so glamorous to us, in conquering which so many billions and billions and billions of dollars and other currencies are spent, if that can be so attractive and so impressive, and so proven in our consciousness, I do not see the difficulty in understanding a similar, why only similar, an expanding concept of expansion itself in a spiritual environment, in the spiritual world. Because the physical universe only expands as we see it. The spiritual universe, maybe there are multi-universes, who can ever say where it is expanding, how far it can expand, where this expansion gets stopped? It cannot stop!

Therefore abhyasis should remember, and we are all abhyasis, we should first remember, you see, and convince ourselves, not mentally and intellectually, but in our hearts, that this is a road which goes on forever and ever. It never stops. It is a journey which will never end. In one sense, if you look upon it in a physical analogical way of a way which must have an end and a destination, "Yes," Babuji said, "there is the goal. There is the destination." But he also said, "It is ever there. And at the Centre, there is only the Ultimate. We are ever approaching nearer and nearer."

So this is necessary that we understand this with our hearts, that we accept it with our hearts; and for me it is a very joyful, very exhilarating idea, a concept, a possibility that, for me, this journey will never end. I will never have that frustration of coming to a point in space or time and saying, "Now it is over, what next?" People who have achieved something in life are very familiar with this frustration, "What next?" A ship owner buys one ship, "What next?" He buys another ship, "What next?" Third ship, "What next?" So this frustration of achievement which we find in the physical world, in our temporal lives, in our temporal existences, is an absolutely certain frustration. You see, nobody can escape it. The one who does not achieve is frustrated because of non-achievement, the one who achieves is frustrated because he does not know what to do next. He says, "What shall I do now? I have come to the top. I am now the chairman of the board of directors. What do I do now?"

So do not forget, sisters and brothers, that frustration is a fact of life, and to ascribe it to non-achievement or to un-success, excuse my playing with the English language, is a fact of existence, is like our shadow which will ever be with us. And if there is one certain way of cutting off that shadow from our existence, it is by axing this desire for achievement in any field, including the spiritual. Because as I say, as I repeat again and again, perhaps *ad nauseum*, the moment we have achieved, we are finished.

So this is the first thing about the method of Sahaj Marg, which our Master has bestowed on us: that the goal is a very specific goal, it is a very definite goal, it exists. Where? Can you give it a location in space and time? Absolutely not. Where then does it reside? As my Master said, "Within yourself." So this is the logic for our meditation, that we do not adopt external symbols or objects of meditation, however exalted they may have been in the past or may be in the future, but we position it, we locate it, we identify it, inside the heart.

Very often people are asked, preceptors are asked, "Why meditation on the heart?" And many of us say, "Well, because Babuji said so," or, "Lalaji said so," but that is not the right

The Master, the Mission, and the Method

answer, you see. Of course, that is part of the answer. They said it. But why did they say it? You see, it is like children, when they get curious about the fact of childbirth, "Mummy, where did I come from?" "Oh, you came from your mother." "And where did mother come from?" "From her mother." Ultimately, you have to say, "Darling, there is such a thing as a God who is the all-mother, you know, and from her, your great-great-great-great-great-grandmother came. So that is one way of answering for a parent who cannot answer, and for a child who is too inquisitive.

So there is no use in saying, "Babuji said because Lalaji said." All right, why did Lalaji say it? There is a reason why they said it. And the reason is this: that in the heart is the goal of human existence. Not outside, but within! "Seek within and you shall find. My kingdom is not of this world." I mean, all these things have been said before, you see, but we have just understood them either intellectually or emotionally. And then we make the same tragic mistake of locating that Ultimate in a place of worship, and going there to find it, or in a place of pilgrimage, and suffering the tortures of the body and the spirit to go there and find whatever you think you are going to find — and ultimately discovering that all these promises are like the fool's gold at the end of a rainbow. It is supposed to be there, but is never found.

Then the miracle happens, if you have the ability, if you have the genius, of acceptance. It is really a genius, you see, to accept what a master says, unproven by any logic, unproven by any substantiated body of knowledge, unproven by any systematic research, to accept it and to go ahead. And the proof of that Master's greatness, the efficacy of his system, the verity of his words, the largeness of his heart, the immensity of his love, is that so many of us are here today. Who could ever have dreamt that on European soil there would be so many preceptors! I do not think, even in India, I have had so many preceptors at a meeting. Last Basant, we had a hundred and thirty-three, I think, perhaps that was the largest number ever.

So you see, the proof of a thing is in the **presence** of something, not in the fact that it has been proved to be. Science proves by other means, you see, that a man was sitting here because certain infrared or whatever vibrations show that there is a depression, which must have been pressed there by a certain body. It is verification, which is always after the fact. Science proves by verification. Spirituality proves by the immediate presence of the thing, which must be, and which has been, and which shall eternally be there: myself, yourself, the Self. So this is why we seek within, notwithstanding what the great religions may say.

Unfortunately, the religions have said the same thing, or at least the founders have said the same thing. But then, you know, the successors build temples and the temples become, shall we say, the *abattoirs* of spirituality; very satisfying, sometimes we can relieve ourselves of our loads of sin and guilt, which is a very temporary catharsis of the mind. As Babuji once said, rather crudely as he himself said, he said, "Forgive me, I am using a very crude and vulgar example, you see. But we should not use spiritual sadhana like we use a toilet, to relieve ourselves." As far as I know, all traditions have been such places. You go there once a week, once a month or whenever you feel the need, say something, do something, give something, and come back feeling lightened. Perhaps the lightness is real, perhaps it is ephemeral, perhaps it is illusory. It does not last long in any case. That is why today we find this peculiar phenomenon that religions are failing in their ability to get people to come to worship, and all sorts of concessions are being made, to even morality, for instance. So when that happens, and when the standards are lowered to enable people

The Master, the Mission, and the Method

to come who are already of much lesser standards in their personal living, what is it going to fulfil?

So the turn towards spirituality is, I think, inevitable. It is not something that we choose, or something which we want to do, or not want to do. It is absolutely inevitable. Because in the historical process of the development of cultures, of civilizations, of religions, if there is one proof, it is this proof: that in all these fields where man, or the human being, has externalized the symbols of his power, his possessiveness, his happiness, his contentment, his joy, it is doomed to failure. It is doomed to frustration. This is the lesson that the history of civilization teaches us, the history of religions teaches us; or if it has not taught you yet, it **should** teach you. And what is necessary to accept that teaching? An open mind. If there is prejudice, and if you say, "Well, this fellow is a salesman you know. He is selling Sahaj Marg. That is what he will say. But my God has said..." And the moment he says, "My God," well, I would hear a groan from God, if there is a God to groan. He would say, "What is this 'my God'? Does this fellow have the temerity, the arrogance, the cheek, to claim me as his own?"

So, putting it rather bluntly, we have to learn this lesson. I mean, if culture is there, it is to teach us something. It is to teach us to be refined. Culture is an emanation of human refinement. Morality is the actualization of a human being's moral standards of existence. We do not **follow** morality, you see. Morality comes out of our living, out of our behaviour, out of the way we handle our environment. So to look upon morality as a body of do's and don'ts, rules, and then to be plagued by the sense of guilt that I have done something which a body of knowledge says, "Thou shalt not do," is stupid. There is morality because there were people who lived in that way. And we look at their lives and say, "This is worth emulation, this is the standard of ideal, the ideal of perfection that I should follow." What did they do? We codify it and a body of morals, a body of teaching, emerges out of their existence.

So teachings are not created by human thought. Please remember this, because in the Occident there is this tradition that knowledge is taught. I would prefer to say: knowledge emanates. In the original sense, yes, everything is given. But only in the original condition, at the origin of time, of the universe, of existence itself. Subsequently it is **given** to us. What my Master taught is my knowledge, where else could I get it from? I did not learn it in schools. Where did he get it from? It was given to him by the example of his Master's living, his Master's teachings, which he followed with an incorruptibility of the soul, with an absoluteness of dedication, with an unswerving loyalty to the goal that he had set for himself. And with, shall we say, a love which could not sway hither or thither. And therefore, his Master became for him, the ideal, the perfect God. Therefore he could write in *Voice Real* with courage, conviction, and say, "Which God ever took pity on this insignificant being? If someone took pity on me, it was my Master and my Master alone. And if I ever saw God, it was because of my Master. To whom should I therefore be grateful? To God, or to my Master?" Question mark — no answer. Well, the answer is implicit in the question, you see.

One thing I learned from my Master, "It is only a fool who seeks an answer outside a question." Many of you who have been associated with him, Babuji, know that he always said, "The question contains its own answer." Look within the question, you see. But we have been taught by the systems of moral education, to look outside for things, including for answers to questions. Therefore, this ideal of a human who could be perfect, who could be Divine, emerges not from a body of knowledge which says, "There **shall** be." It comes from one who **is**, whom we follow, and we say, "Yes, this is for me

The Master, the Mission, and the Method

the ideal, the perfect, none other than this do I know! None other than this can I ever know! If I ever know it, it is only through Him. Therefore, He is the Ultimate for me."

So you see, the search now becomes a little changed from the heart, where we had an abstract notion of Divinity, an abstract presence which we could never identify, a very real presence but which we could never feel, and a voice which ever spoke to us but which we never heard. All this we now transfer, it is a real transference of all these things, from one's heart into the person of the Master. Now, we hear Him as the voice of the conscience who should have spoken to me from inside myself. We love Him as the Ultimate which I should have loved, within myself, in its Eternal Presence. We seek Him as the God whom I know has existed for ever and anon in my heart, but whom I could not find. So you see, it is an exteriorization of the Ultimate Principle which **was** ever in us, which **is** ever in us, which **shall ever be** in us, for the purpose of being able to grasp it physically with our understanding, emotionally with our love, spiritually with ultimate success.

So the Master is an instrument for our evolution. It is not something we should fantasize about, "What is a Master? Who should be a Master? Why a Master?" Why a Master? Because we need one! If I could have done this without the need for a Master outside myself, to speak to me from outside what he could not tell me from inside, not because he was incapable of saying it, but because I was a stupid deaf idiot! I need him to show me things which I should have seen with my heart, but which I was too blind to see until he showed them with his eyes through my eyes, the knowledge which I have ever contained within myself. Because if that knowledge is not ever within me, I do not exist. Please take this as a **fact**. I do not exist because I am, I am because I **exist**. I am always a little annoyed with this business of "*Cogito ergo sum.*" (I think, therefore I am.)

The man who said that was much less than wise. "I **am**, therefore I think." A corpse cannot say, "*Cogito ergo sum.*" I mean, this simple logic seems to have defeated the Occidental mind of those days. I hope it does not continue to defeat us! So you see, it is from this 'I am', you see. And who is the 'I'? Well, until I find Him inside me, it is the Master. Therefore it is the Master who is 'me'! "I am the Master." We cannot say that, but the Master is 'me'.

Therefore in our spiritual technique of meditation, Babuji has said, "If you find it difficult to meditate, think I am sitting where you are sitting and I am meditating." Everything becomes possible when you think he is doing it. And as a preceptor, when I was made a preceptor way back in 1967, the first advice he gave to me was, "If you find any difficulty in the work, think I am sitting there, make this thought strong, that it is conviction, not merely a thought. If necessary feel that there is a beard on your face, and you will find the work goes well." And it does go well. I have found that, whenever I thought I was giving the sitting, it was much less than what it should have been. And when I was able to remove myself, erase my presence from there, the miracle of Babuji's presence happens and the sitting is perfect. You cannot categorize it as good, or satisfying. The only words that you can use to express it, "It is perfect."

So perfection comes through Him, you see, perfection can never be ours. Now, this is a concept which can be obnoxious to the European mind, where we are trained to seek perfection in what we do, "Yes, I want to do something which is perfect." The painter wants something perfect, the artist wants something perfect, the architect wants to build the perfect house. But when we think it is here in me, the perfection — we fail. Babuji always said, "Perfection is only in God," in the sense that He is perfect, everything that comes from Him is perfect, every-

The Master, the Mission, and the Method

thing He does is perfect. In us, we are human, we have these limitations of the self, we have the limitations imposed on us by education, by culture, by nationality, so many things, you see. So when we think, "I am doing something," it is miserable. When we think, "He is doing something," with the heart, feeling his presence — it is a miracle!

So the need for the Master is the second need, you see. First, that he becomes the exteriorization of all the ideals that I should have, which are in me but which I cannot recognize, which I cannot find. It is like a man wearing his spectacles and hunting frantically for them on the table top, until his wife tells him, "Look here." [pointing to the head] So the Master here [pointing to the heart], we make him; we create the Master, you see. In a sense, the Master is a creation of ourselves. "He comes when needed." What does it mean? "Knock and it shall be open unto thee?" No! Sit in your house and pray with devotion. He knocks at your door. This is, if you permit a slight invertendo again, the invertendo of religion and spirituality. There, you have to knock and somebody says, "*Entrez*," you know, and you have to go in. Here, I am sitting at peace in my house, awaiting my beloved, and He comes. He knocks, and I have to open the door for Him. He is Almighty, He is Ultimate, He is Divine. Nevertheless He is courteous enough to respect my privacy, to respect my need for Him, and says, "When you need me, call me, I shall be there. Think of me, I shall be there." I do not think there exists any human lover who could say that.

So you see, I am not in any sense trying to philosophize, or fantasize, or to play with words when I say, "The Master is our creation." Because if I do not accept him as a Master, to me, at least, he is no Master. Babuji used to live in Shahjahanpur, and even his neighbours did not know about him. For them he was an old man who was a clerk in the Courts of Shahjahanpur, retired on a small pension, and, because of his age, they would say *namaste* when he came out, nothing more. So, if that something is next to us, in front of us, staring us in the face, it does not mean, automatically, that we are going to recognize its presence, accept it and use it. Acceptance is an act of the heart, not of the mind.

The mind plays so many tricks. It can ask, "Why a human being? Is not my Christ enough, or is not my Buddha enough, or is not my Krishna enough? Why a Ram Chandra?" you see, all over again. It can say, "Why an Indian, why not a European? I am German. Why not a German guru?" "I am Dutch. Why not a Dutch guru?" "I am South African, why not a South African guru?" We are Indians and South Africans, God is not Indian or South African. He is the Creator. It is like asking the owner of the palace, "Majesty, where is your room?" He will say, "My friend, you are my guest, this is **your** room. The palace is mine; the kingdom is mine; the world is mine; the universe is mine!" So, to have located such a person in a time-space framework is worse than stupid. And what can be more stupid than even that? To demand that a master should come out of such and such a time and motion framework, or time and space framework, or such and such a geographical, national, socio-economic, political framework — this is the mistake that most people make, everywhere in the world. Indians do it as much as Europeans, because the human temperament, the human nature is unchanged, you see. We are all human beings. Scratch us and we are human beings, it is only the surface which is black or white.

So this lesson, you know, that the Master is a person we need; he must be the exteriorization of all that we hold dear and divine within our hearts, but which we do not know anything about, and that I must accept him totally as such. "Love thy neighbour as thyself." Love Master as yourself, because if you love yourself you stop your progress for the reason I stated

The Master, the Mission, and the Method

before, just as we started this talk. Love Him, the miracle happens that you still love the Self, which is in you, which is Him, and your progress is faster because now you love that which you want to follow, you love that which you want to emulate, you love that whom you wish to respect, to adore, who is your ideal, whom you want to become like.

So this is the subtle, you know, the subtle resonance coming from within. I say 'resonance', because it is to the call of my heart. It is like an echo across the valley. My cry brings the Master to my door, not from outside, but from within me. This is the miracle of the spiritual Master in the Sahaj Marg system, that out of me comes my Master. And him I follow, him I pursue, him I adopt, him I venerate, him I adore, him I love, to him I surrender. And he says, "Look within," and there I find he had always been there, and it was His Grace, it was His blessing, that he was able to clear the rubbish from my vision, clear the wax out from my ears, clear the screen from my understanding, and I see him inside, you see, and the outside Master is only a reflection of what is inside. Now when I leave the mirror, and walk away, the image may fail but the reality is going. It cannot be lost! Even if the mirror is broken the reality of my presence cannot be lost.

Then comes this ultimate miracle, you see, that if in this process we have been successful, of total acceptance, total surrender, total love for him, and he creates this miracle of clearing my perceptions, spiritual, temporal, anything, you see, and making me see him inside, now the need for his external presence vanishes. I do not need a mirror any more to show me my face. I know my face, I know my Self, with a capital 'S'. I have seen Him outside so that I could recognize Him inside, the miracle has occurred, I brought Him out of myself, He put himself back within me and says, "Now be happy. Now be content. The way is within you. The Master is within you. The goal is within you. Pursue it unflaggingly, with determination, because all is not ONE yet." "Why?" you may ask. "If He is within you, why?" Because, eventually, this idea that He is within me should also go. Because He is still a presence which is distinct from my own self. He is still something to whom I look as someone separate, other than myself, a voice from within me which is not my voice, you see.

So that is why we have this teaching of the ultimate state of spiritual fulfilment, which is called mergence with the Master. Thereafter there is no Master within, there is no Master without. He **is**. You cannot say **what** He is, you cannot say **where** He is, you cannot say **why** He is, you cannot even say **when** He is. Was He in the past? Nay, He is in the future. Not in the present? Of course, in the present too! Therefore such a person becomes eternal, His presence becomes eternal, He is ever and always.

So this is a broad sort of sketch of what is meditation, why we meditate, what the heart is, why we should meditate on the heart. And the need to transfer our allegiance, spiritual or emotional allegiance, from externalized symbols of divinity, to a living, pulsating thing, you know, which can be brought out from a living pulsating thing into the outside, put back again. It is not that there is no God outside, you see. If God is infinite, if God is immutable, if God is all-pervasive everywhere, He must be everywhere. Outside too! Spirituality only says, "When He is inside, why do you look for Him outside?"

So we have no quarrels with religions, you see. Religions say, "He is here." [pointing outward] We say, "He is here too." [pointing inside] They say, "Come to me for worship." We can say, with confidence, with candour, with absolute truth, "I prefer to worship Him within myself. Here He is ever mine, ever inseparable from me, my existence, the source of my

The Master, the Mission, and the Method

existence, the source of all benignity, beatitude, that can possibly be showered upon me, showering from inside." Why should I seek Him outside? In seeking Him outside, I live a lie, I deny the truth of spiritual existence, I deny His presence within. To seek Him outside, such a God will say, "Well, go ahead, the universe is vast! When you have searched for Him everywhere and you have not found Him then come back to me in your own heart and look for me there, there shall I reveal myself to you."

So it is not that spirituality denies religion or negates religion, it only transcends religion. It makes all those expensive troublesome journeys avoidable. It says the same truth I am telling you. What they are saying, I am saying. If God is in every atom, He is in every atom of your body. If He is everywhere, surely He is in you. If there is a temple for Him, surely your heart is a temple too. Why do you not worship Him in this temple, within you, which you carry ever with you, which you do not have to look for, where no doors have to be opened, no priest has to officiate, no offerings have to be made, no sacrifice is demanded? That is **all** that spirituality says, and that is **enough** that should be said. What more should we say? And when we do this, people often ask, "What are the socio-political, economical benefits?" Well, if I can find Him in my heart, what more do I need if I find existence itself embodied in myself?

It is like asking a pregnant woman, "Yes, you are pregnant, what have you got?" She says, "What have I got? I have my baby! What more do I need? Something I have been longing for, waiting for, it is mine. I created it, it is mine!" Fortunately, even the men can say now, "This is mine, you see, this is **my** God, I created Him, I found Him, I structured Him with the help of the Master whom I created from myself out, and whom I put back in. He is my God; He is a God of my creation; He is my creation itself." Now, you have to understand the two senses there, you see. That He creates me, and I create Him because I lost touch with Him, lost sight of Him, lost the knowledge of His presence, the experience of His presence. And therefore the spiritual journey has to be made to find Him where He was always. So if you understand these things, again I say, "with your heart," you will find, you know, we have no quarrel with any convictions, or with any bodies, or systems of knowledge, or truth, or worship, or philosophy. We only say, "Friend, look inside."

I do not know if I am following the agenda but, [he chuckles] [laughter] it is a bad habit of mine. The Master, the Mission, the method, you see, I seem to have covered it, [laughter] knowingly or unknowingly. Then we have to come to the basic elements: prayer, meditation, cleaning, constant remembrance.

I am rather averse to mechanical interpretation of the system, and I think, in our books, we have dealt sufficiently with prayer, meditation, cleaning, and constant remembrance. And if you now understand what I have been saying for the past, well, a little more than half an hour, you will understand one thing, you see, that prayer is also addressed to the Self, here [pointing to the heart]. When we think of a God outside, somewhere in heaven, somewhere far off, who has in His hands the unfortunate power of dispensing justice, or denying it, or withholding it, the power of punishment and reward, we feel frustrated as human beings, and rightly so.

I rebel against a concept of God who can run me like a horse, holding the reins in His hands you see, and the rowels plowing into my sides. I absolutely rebel at such a concept. Because on the one hand we say that God is love, and on the other we say he has condemned us to twenty thousand years or

The Master, the Mission, and the Method

two hundred thousand years, or the millennia to follow in hell. You have only to read Dante's *Inferno* to see the horrors of the diseased mind that could conceive of a justice so inhuman, leave alone divine. I do not uphold such teachings as anything except that of a diseased mind, excuse me, when to even conceive of a hell is difficult. When human beings are so merciful that they weep when we see other human beings suffer, when our justice is there which says, "Until a criminal is proved to be a criminal, he shall not be punished," when we are so generous that we are willing to feed stray cats, stray dogs, sparrows with broken wings, how is it possible that God can be so inhuman and create infernos and hells and, you know, all these despicable, dirty, nauseating things? I cannot imagine it.

I have had discussions with Babuji about this, and much to my surprise, he said, "Yes, hell does exist." I was shocked. Even more shocking was his statement that he has never been able to find heaven in spite of all his searching throughout the known universes, in plural! This was a very devastating shock to me, you see. Here I am denying the concept of a hell, of a God who can create a hell, who can be so inhuman as to create places of punishment, and my Master says, "Yes, it exists." Of course, for some time I was very upset. I could not even ask him, "Where is it?" I was annoyed, you know, with Master, that he is sort of trotting out old fears of fire and brimstone and pitch. It may be in any other modified form, you see, but it is something which I could not bear, it is abhorrent to me, you see. But later on, when I discussed with him, he said, "Do not think of all the molten tar that they pour down your throats, and the spears that they put through your eyes for seeing the wrong things. And the molten wax they pour into your ears for hearing the wrong things, it is not like that. It creates a state of giddiness, you see, vertigo." And then he said, "It is not a God which creates that vertigo. Do not think that because there is a hell, there is a God who sends you to hell. It is you who put yourself in that situation and suffer that, which you are in your ignorance, and in a certain way, in a self-satisfying way, ascribing to a God, because it relieves you of the responsibility for being responsible for your own punishment."

You know, the human mind has absolutely fascinating capacity for self-deception. Anything which I do not want, God has done. "What can I do, I have tried anything, you know, but God is blind. This is my destiny. Therefore, you know, I do not go to church, I do not go to a temple any more. Why worship a God who is so inhuman?" But my Master told me this absolutely fascinating truth: that hell exists, it is our creation. We create it for ourselves, there is no such thing as a hell where all condemned souls are sent, you know. It is not a prison, it is not like the Chateau d'If outside Marseilles. It is within me. Why is there no heaven? It is not necessary, you see. I asked Babuji this question, "What about the heaven? Should I not be able to create?" He said, "Not necessary, because when God is within you, you are heaven yourself, why do you need another heaven? You see, a hell you can create, but a heaven you need not create, for it is unnecessary. It is within you. Seek within and find your heaven which you have been searching for."

So you see the spiritual truth, the greatest truth of my Master's teaching: that there is no heaven, because heaven has always been, it is part of me, it is **me**. Therefore we say, "In him, or in her, I found my heaven," or, if you choose, "My haven." "You are my heaven." Why? Because, in you, I find that manifestation of the heavenly divine qualities, the divine effulgence, the divine nature, the love, the generosity, the kindness that we associate with it, and you say, "She is my heaven," or, "It is my heaven." Heaven does not need to be created. Hell is created by our own wrong thoughts, wrong actions, grossness. So if there is a hell, and Babuji has said there

The Master, the Mission, and the Method

is, it must be, it is a creation of our grossness. So when people come to me and say, "Oh, I am suffering the tortures of hell." Of course, we cannot be unkind and say, "Yes, suffer it! Because you have created it." [laughter] We cannot.

To my mind, hope is a heaven in itself, because there is this old English saying, you know, that, "Where there is life, there is hope." Life without hope would be meaningless, it would be a hell in itself. A hopeless life is not a life, it is a stagnation, you see, it is a cesspool, it is a mire in which we have got mired, into which we are sinking deeper and deeper — the quicksands of the negative side of existence. Into that we sink by our own foolishness. We did not know where we were going. We stepped into it and within ten minutes, the last strand of hair has disappeared, and we are just bubbles, you see, being laboriously released by that sand. So, where is heaven, where is hell? Again, they are within us. You see, hell is within us if God is not within us. If you go through the English countryside, you find hunting lodges, old cottages where the kings slept, "Here slept Louis XIV." "Here slept Henry Tudor." Whatever it is, you see. I do not remember the names. And the old saying, "Where the king is, that is a palace! Where God is, that is a temple." But we make a temple and look for God there. And we build a palace and look for a king within, and we find a fool occupying the throne. It is not his fault.

So spirituality says, "If there is the Divine in you, and if He is everything, for heaven's sake, how can that which is inside you not be the God, and therefore that which is in you not be heaven itself, or the Heaven of heavens?" I contain heaven inside me. I mean we should all have this capacity to say this loud and bold, you see, "What are you looking for ye people of the earth?" You know, in a sort of spirit of conversion, if you have the gift, soap box opera, the Hyde Park, you know, stand on top of a packing case and shout, "Where are you looking? Look inside!" Nobody will listen to you. "Look inside for what? My heart? Yes, I know, the poor thing is weak, you know. It will not even beat properly. What do you expect me to look for? I am going to my doctor." Yes. Who made it like that? Who put grossness, who covered it with an alligator-tough skin so that it cannot even blub-blub properly? Because it has lost that elasticity, you see. Doctors ascribe it to cholesterol, or some such other idiosyncratic principle. What about the grossness which creates cholesterol, that creates fatty acids, that creates all the things with which you are lining your tubes and vesicles? This we forget, you see, and then we go to doctors, dietitians, homoeopaths, quacks, astrologers, I Ching, Tao, Tarots. What for? Again we are looking outside for the knowledge that we have within us, and we suffer because they do not have the knowledge that is within me. In me is absolute knowledge. They speak from what knowledge they have derived, faultily, incompletely, through education. Education never completes our education. It is a well-known truth, you see. I mean, it is an education in itself to find out that education does not educate, not completely, by any means. So what are we going to them for? So spirituality says, "Even for that, look inside. You cannot find out, go to the Master, he will tell you what is wrong with you." And you go to Babuji, you know, expecting volumes of truth to spew out of his mouth, and he looks very profoundly at you for a few seconds, and says, "I am telling you, it is all grossness." [laughter] This happened to me the first time I went to Shahjahanpur, I had been used to some other gurus, you know, who could speak, like I am speaking now, for hours at a time [laughter], talking a great deal but saying very little.

    I expected something like that with my Master and I had spent nearly two hours next to him. All that I heard was the beautiful, delightful sound of his hookah. I think he smoked

The Master, the Mission, and the Method

the hookah just to lull us into thinking that we are hearing something. [laughter] You see, this is not a joke. I mean it in a very real sense. Because to most human beings, silence is intolerable. We cannot be silent, we cannot 'be in silence' — two things which we have to learn. And this again, the system that my Master teaches: close your eyes, close your mouth, bring your limbs together, so that they are not active, sit in a comfortable position, look inside, try to hear His voice. And Babuji has said, "That voice is so feeble now, because we have never listened to it." It is like a dog which barks and barks and you never listen, it lies down and goes to sleep. And we try to remove all the impediments to that hearing, like you close your doors, draw your curtains when you are listening to music, so that there should be no outside disturbance. Here, we have to close the doors of our senses, bolt them securely, look inside. Still we do not hear. Why? As Babuji said in one word: grossness. You see, it is like a lamp, the glass chimney of which has been coated with soot from inside. The lamp is burning but there is no light coming out. So this is the thing of which Babuji used to say, "Even criminals have this light within them." We do not see it because they have enshrouded it within that enormous solidity of the grossness that they have accumulated. When you clean it away you find the light is still within them, too.

Therefore in Sahaj Marg we are taught, I mean, Babuji insists that, while we can hate what a man does, or a woman does, do not hate the person himself or herself because the person is always divine. For the nonce there is something wrong with it, because it is covered over with slime, with mud. Clean it away and it is as pure as you are. I remember a great statement attributed to Swami Vivekananda that, "Every Buddha is a worm evolved, and every worm is a Buddha involved, in itself."

So this generosity, you know, of conception, that criminals, prostitutes, philosophers, saints — in essence they are the same. See, this question arose when I asked Babuji the question, "What is the qualification to be an abhyasi?" He said, "Your willingness." I said, "Not my qualities?" He said, "Well, if I were to tell you the truth, you would be shocked." [laughter] I said, "Yes, please tell me, I wish to be shocked." He said, "There is very little difference between the highest evolved human being and the lowest human being." I said, "Very little difference? Then what am I coming to you for?" He said, "For that very little difference [laughter], without which you are what you are, but with which you shall be what you have to be." So for that little difference, we are working so much, you see. And what is that little difference? One is gross, the other is not gross. One is gross, the other is subtle. One is human, one is divine. The essence is ever the same.

So you see this generosity, this magnificent open-heartedness, where a Master can say, "My heart is the playing ground for all of humanity." Religion does not say it. No religion has said this. They say, "Come to me, worship me, follow me. I am the truth. Me alone shall you find!" Isn't it? At least the two great religions have said it. Hinduism has escaped because it was like the amoeba which absorbs everything into itself — a very intelligent way of doing things. But this magnificence, this generosity, this love, you see, this humanity — that we are essentially the one, though there are differences in the way we manifest ourselves, you see.

What is behaviour but the way in which we manifest ourselves? What is knowledge that we speak about, but the way in which we allow the inner knowledge of the Ultimate to manifest itself through our mouth? So when these are limited, the Infinite within me I limit in its manifestation by my sensory instruments, by my desires, by my conception of what I am. If

The Master, the Mission, and the Method

a doctor thinks, "I am a doctor," well, he may be a very good doctor, but it is a limit. My profession is that of a doctor, you see, but I am a human being. I am a Sahaj Marg abhyasi, I hope to be perfect. Yes, we have to be something, we have to earn our livings, one is a doctor, one is a banker, one is a hawker — why not? But these things should not in any way negate or stultify the inner thing that seeks to express itself through me.

And if spirituality ultimately achieves its objective, it is precisely this miracle of total expression of my inside through my outside, you see. What Babuji meant by living a balanced existence. "What you speak you shall mean, what you mean you shall speak." What does it mean? Now we intend to say something, we say something else. We desire to say something, we say something else. We have to be polite, we have to be courteous, we have to be civilized, you see. Therefore, spirituality says, "Beware of this civilization." Civilization thrusts hypocrisy upon you in the way of culture, in the way of manners, in the way of behaviour. These are veneers you are putting on to yourself, they are masks, they are not yourself. Does it mean Babuji had no value for civilization? Not at all, you see. He had the highest value for civilization, but a civilization which flows from inside. Not as a veneer imposed upon you by society, by knowledge, by education, by culture, but something which springs out of you like the spring waters come out from the bowels of the earth, you see, spring, crystal clear source. I must allow my source to flow out of me, you see. Which means, when such a man speaks it is divine, when he says something it is divine, when he talks it is divine, when he walks it is divine — everything that he does. Because, it is not he who is doing it, it is the inner spring in him which is welling out through him. And this is possible only by cleaning away the samskaras, and transmitting to him the essence of the Master which we have all been permitted to do.

So you see, the essence of spiritual existence is this: the ability, or acquiring the ability, to erase, to efface myself, so that that which is within me shall flow out of me in all its effulgence, in its divinity. So what is it that you are talking of becoming and achieving and getting and grasping? All this becomes senseless, you see. That is why, perhaps in one of my talks in Vorauf, I said, "Evolution, it has no meaning, you see, I am not evolving into something." Perhaps I should say, I am devolving from that which I have become into that which I was. That would be a greater truth, a more acceptable truth. So this is what we try to do.

And now we have the Master, we have the method. What is the Mission? Well, it is an organized body, which can offer the Master's teachings, his practice, to what Babuji always referred to as a 'suffering humanity'. We need something, you know; when you wish to speak to somebody, you need a telephone, it is an organization. When you need to go somewhere, you need a train or a plane; it is an organization. It is an organization which runs these benefits for our use: services, utilities. But when it comes to spirituality, people argue, you see, "Oh, why an organization? Why an ashram? Why a Shri Ram Chandra Mission? We do not like organization in Europe, because so many organizations are corrupt." Yes of course, but your body is an organization! You have a heart, a pair of lungs, the liver, the stomach, the large intestines, the small ones, I mean, Gertie can run through the list later. [laughter] What for? It is an organization, you see.

If you study the body, it is said that every cell has its own independent existence. It comes into being, it dies. But my existence is independent of the millions and billions of cells which have their own independent existence within me. 'I' am one, I say. But I am also billions of things, which are growing within me, dying within me, are being born within me. If you

The Master, the Mission, and the Method

look at it that way, each of you is a universe in yourself, you see, and there is a ruling God within yourself; and perhaps the organisms which are within you, growing and being born, and dying, loving, hating, all this phenomena of existence, perhaps they look to you, inside you, as the god who is ruling them!

So we are cheating those billions of things which are within us too, you see, when we deny its existence. Suppose you worship a God and God was to come and say, "My dear, you know, I am no God. Forgive me, you see, I have been this, that and the other." You would be shattered! What happens to my organism when I deny God? I suffer, I die, not because 'I' die, but because all that which constitutes me dies. Because their god is being destroyed in the process.

So you see, an organization must exist, and the organization must have a presiding deity. My heart is the presiding organism for my body. That which is within that heart is the thing which governs. If I deny it from outside, I deny it from inside, my organization collapses. 'I' really die then, you see. Perhaps you can use this analogy to see why we need an organization like a mission.

I have said in the past, I repeat it again, a mission is not a structure of brick and mortar, it is that which we adopt as the purpose of our life. "What is your mission in life?" you are asked. "My mission is my Master's Mission." "What is his Mission?" "His Master's Mission." "What was it?" To offer to humanity, in words of my Master, 'suffering humanity', a simple, universally acceptable, easily practicable system of practice which, in a short space of time, will enable them to find within themselves what they have been desperately, stupidly, unsuccessfully seeking outside.

So that is all I have to say for this morning. I hope I have covered something of the agenda. But you know, I am like one

Courmettes

of those Indians who find it difficult to stay on the road [he chuckles] [laughter] and keep veering from the left to the right and the right to the left. But it is fun while it lasts. [laughter]

3

The Role of the Master

Courmettes, France
Monday, July 11, 1988

I will start off with something about prayer. I think way back in 1972, in the days of brother Andre Poray, we had a meeting in Sanary, Jean-Michel Piquemal will remember it, and the others of you who were members then. And there was a great deal of discussion about prayer, not because people did not know what prayer is or they did not want to pray, but out of a feeling of revulsion from the traditional church.

Now that was something which was, at the same time, worrying and amusing. Because it showed a certain lack of ability to judge the merit of a thing, in itself, for itself. That religious systems have misused prayers or prayer, does not mean that prayer is by itself a bad thing, or an undesirable thing, or a corrupt thing. And we must also remember that it is we who prayed, whether under the over-all tutelage of a church, or of a lesser entity of the family. And when we prayed, we prayed because we needed to. We must always remember why we pray. Then only can we understand whether it is necessary in our existence or not.

Babuji Maharaj was quite, I would not say confused, because he was never confused, but he could not understand the then European attitude to prayer. He said, "Why are they so upset about prayer? What is it that they object to?" I said, "But Babuji Maharaj, you also say prayer is begging." He said, "Yes, of course, in the normal way when we do nothing but ask, and ask, and ask. We certainly have a right to ask for that

39

which we need, not which we want." You see, Babuji was very specific in drawing a very subtle, very fine, but very deliberate and necessary distinction between needs and wants. His philosophy says that we have a right to the needs of existence. The wants are created by us. And it was his very forthright, downright, unambiguous, often repeated statement that we never pray for our needs, we pray for our wants. And he said this is why it is called begging. And he used to elaborate, I mean in a semi-humorous way, semi-critical way, semi-caustic manner, that God, who is characterized as all love, merciful, compassionate, He does not deny the basic needs of existence to any of His creation. Water, air to breathe, the basic necessities of life as we call them, these are assured whether we are animals, birds, insects. Of course, somebody who wants to be rather dogmatic and argumentative can say, "What about the Sahel and the Sahara and places like that? Where is God's mercy there?" It would be well to remember that those deserts are largely the creation of human cupidity, covetousness, avarice, greed, selfishness.

So, prayer as something we indulge in, the word indulge I deliberately use, is something which Babuji looked upon as obnoxious, in the sense that we are asking for more and more. And you all know his story about the great Moghul emperor who was praying in his private prayer house, and a saint wanted audience with him. He was stopped at the gate of the palace. He said, "I am a holy man." The door-keeper said, "My Master, the emperor, is praying." He said, "Well, he is involved in a holy act, I am a holy man, so I do not see any objection to going there." He was permitted to go. When he came into the prayer chamber, he found this great Moghul emperor asking God for more territories, more victories, more of this, more of that. He must have been nauseated. The greatest emperor of those times, begging on his knees for more. As he got up to go away, the emperor turned round and said, "Wait, I am just finishing, I will attend to you as soon as I finish my prayers." The saint said, "No! No! You see, I am building an ashram, and I thought I would come and ask you for some financial assistance, but I find you are yourself a beggar. What can I beg from a beggar? And if at all I have to beg, I will beg from Him from whom you are begging." I mean it is a point with a great moral behind it, that even emperors are beggars.

That is why my Master used to say, I mean, excuse me for repeating it; sometimes the rich people get annoyed that I appear to make them the targets of my talks; it is not so, you see; it is a philosophy. There is a moral to be drawn from these stories which I heard from my Master. He said, "It is an amazing thing, Parthasarathi, that the poor do not beg. It is the rich who beg. And the richer they are, the more they beg for."

So this is another principle of invertendo that the needy do not beg, they just surrender to existence, you see. You find them in the poor countries of the world, they are lying by the side of the street, too poor even to beg, too weak even to ask, even from God. They say, "Well if this is your will, so let it be done." It is, therefore, in the poor of the world that you find this attitude of surrender. You may say, "Well, it is an enforced surrender." Why not? Surrender, in whichever way it comes, is desirable. And if you have to be poor and made to suffer before you can surrender, that is also one of the ways of God, one of the ways of destiny. In fact it is one of the ways that the individual soul has evolved for itself from its experience arising out of its previous life. Because this is the great truth, that when a soul leaves this embodied existence, Babuji used to say, "The moment we die, we become all wisdom," because in that state in the hereafter, the limbo between two lives, there can be no foolishness. It is all wisdom, all love, all clarity, divine, just. There, the soul which has just left its embodied existence ruminates on itself, you see, meditates, "What have I done? What is the negative? What is the positive? What are the plus points? What have I now to do to evolve further on the path of evolution?" And there it decides. You know, there is no God who thrusts it into hell or heaven. As I said yesterday, it is right here in us. This soul decides, in its absolute wisdom, in that limbo of disembodied state: as such and such, in such and such a place, will I take my next birth.

Therefore, please remember that if there is a beggar, that soul which is in the body of the beggar chose to be a beggar, knowing in its wisdom, in its prenatal wisdom, post-mortem wisdom, that in that state only it could evolve. Unfortunately, once we are here our wisdom is clouded, the original wisdom which dictated that I have to be born in such in such a situation, out of such and such parents, in such and such a linguistic area, is forgotten. The need for it is forgotten. We get sort of buffeted, you know, by desires, by the environment, by culture, by tradition, by religion itself. Then we lose this purpose and we start begging.

So this is a very necessary thing to remember, that we are not punished or rewarded by any god in heaven, or by any devil in hell. It is our own doing. And it is not a foolishness that we do, it is not something stupid that we are doing. It is out of that immense wisdom of accumulated existence of umpteen lives that we have led, which are summed up in that moment after death, and which dictates my next life. One who is able to retain that wisdom, albeit in a subconscious or super-conscious fashion, he makes of this life what it should be, the last step on his evolutionary path to the goal. Otherwise, it is but one more out of many steps. So you see, if that is the case, what is the logic in my asking or appealing to any god? Or, for that matter, to any demon or devil, selling my soul to the devil. Both are impossible, you see. Because at least in the East, in India, it is

The Role of the Master

a firm conviction, it is not just a belief, it is a conviction arising out of the personal experience of the saints, that I am the destiny maker for myself. There is no use appealing to an external agency, even to Divinity itself, because I have chosen my destiny. I have chosen my existence, and it is for me to use this existence to further my interest.

So you see, prayer becomes meaningless if you view it in that larger context of how we are born, why we are born, where we are born. That is one way of looking at prayer. The other thing is, notwithstanding Babuji saying, "Prayer is begging," he still advocated prayer. We have a Mission prayer, you see, which everybody is supposed to repeat once in the morning, "O Master, thou art the real goal of human life," you know, in various languages. So I asked Babuji, "Why this prayer? If prayer is begging." Then, as I told you, I think, last year in Vorauf, perhaps, it is also printed in one of the books, I do not want to repeat that all over again here, there are three statements contained in the prayer. The first line states who and what is my goal. And it is the real goal, you see, there can be so many spurious goals, false goals, temporary goals, glittering goals. What is my real goal? "Thou art the real goal of human life." The next line is an illustration of what I am at this moment. "We are yet but slaves of wishes putting bar to our advancement." The third line makes a statement: by your grace alone I can reach it, "Thou art the only God and power to bring us up to that stage." So Babuji said, "Do not misunderstand this prayer, it is not asking, it is not begging, it is nothing of that sort. It is you reminding yourself every morning of your goal, of the purpose of your existence, of your present condition, and trying to remember Him who alone can lead you to that stage which you want to achieve. It is just a statement of fact, it is a remembrance."

Courmettes

Then the next question: "You tell us to pray sometimes. Somebody is sick, you say, pray to Master. What should we do?" He said, "Pray," I said, "In what way? Pray means again it is a begging. Even if I should ask for the life of somebody dear who is dying, is it not a begging?" Then he enunciated that famous principle, you know, to me at least, that when you ask for yourself it is begging, when you ask for somebody else it is never begging. We have a right, I mean it is a right, perhaps even a duty cast upon us by love itself, that when we love we have to ask for those whom we love. We are never allowed to ask for ourselves. So you see, there is a fine distinction between praying for oneself which is begging for oneself and praying for another which is a prayer to the Almighty, "God bestow your mercy on him," or "Master bless him, or her." There is no difference, you see. So that is another aspect of prayer.

Then why pray before meditation? I mean it is neither this nor that. He said it is the way of connecting yourself at one instant of time to the Almighty whose guidance, whose help, you are seeking. And if that is done effectively your meditation becomes something sublime, something effective.

So this is a broad summation of what prayer is. And we should try to give up either our love for religion and our inability to get out of those traps which religion has laid for us, very emotional, very demanding traps, while we should also learn to give up our hatred of those things: revulsion for church, revulsion for the church rituals, revulsion for the church itself, because the church deserves neither. It is an organized institution founded for a certain purpose, like a telephone exchange. If I want it, I use it. If I do not want it, I do not use it. I cannot say, "Take out this telephone exchange because I do not use it." It is for those who need it. It has a purpose, it has a place in existence. All are not so evolved that they can come to the feet of the Master.

The Role of the Master

In fact Babuji once explained to me about the role of the temples in India. You know, you may have a few churches here and there, scattered in Europe. We have hundreds of thousands of temples. I mean you stumble and fall against a temple in India. So I asked Babuji, "What about these temples?" He said they had a purpose. You see, a temple, according to Babuji, was a place where a man could go and worship God whose evolutionary level did not qualify him for the grace of a master, who could never reach a master, who could never approach a master because he could not even know what a master is. His evolutionary level precluded the possibility of either knowing, or understanding, or seeking out a master. So the great saints of the past, in their immense generosity, mercy, love for humanity, they created this system of temple worship, put a form there and charged it. It is that charge which comes out of the temple idol.

And the next great truth which I learned from Master was that this charge has a specific life, lifespan in time, depending on the spiritual approach of the original saint who charged that form of worship, or idol. Obviously, you see, like you have your pencil torchlights, four hours, then you have to recharge again. Suppose a man in the African jungles, you know, a voodoo worshiper, puts that battery and says, "This is the source of all power," what will you get after four hours? Nothing! That is why you find in India this enchanting spectacle, that on one side you have temples where millions, literally millions, of people worship every year; and there are temples almost next door to such temples where the inhabitants are only the owls and the bats. And Babuji said, "This is the proof of what I am saying. There is nothing left there. Human beings have at least this much sensitivity not to go there, because there is nothing there, the charge has become exhausted."

Then Dr. K.C. Varadachari further explained from the theory of atomic disintegration, you see, where we have the half-life periods of certain atoms which can run to thousands or millions of years, and certain atoms which disintegrate in millionths, one millionth of a second. So like that the charge is there. When it is there, there is some purpose in worshiping because you get something in its presence. You have to be there to receive the charge, obviously. So temple worship had a meaning, had effect in those days when these saints were able to charge the idol. Today perhaps nobody exists who can do the charging. So that is why temple worship is as useless as worship in church. I do not know if at any stage in Christianity's history there existed someone who could charge a cross, for instance. So you see, if there is a charge there is some meaning in going there. And that too for whom? Only for one who has no guru.

The guru is the living God. This is the concept of guru in the Hindu tradition, in what we call the *sanathana dharma* tradition, in the yogic tradition. Beyond Him there exists no God. He is not only the object of worship, He is the object of everything. Therefore, Master said, if at all one has to pray, and one has a Master of calibre who is serving his needs, there is some purpose in praying to that Master.

You see, I was asked a question sometime last year. Babuji himself has written that ultimately He [pointing upwards] is the real Master, you see, and all the human Masters who come on this world, on this earth, are His representatives. If that is so, then why do we address the prayer, "O Master" and not "Oh God". Now today I am giving you the answer for that. Because God, it is a living God who is before you in the form of the Master; not that God is dead elsewhere, but this is an embodied flesh-and-blood divinity, you see, who can understand our needs; who can understand our temperaments; who can sym-

The Role of the Master

pathize with us, being human himself; who can accept our failings, perhaps having failed himself in some way.

You know, it is like in a school, the brilliant teachers are generally tyrants. They petrify the students. But the teacher who has himself stumbled and fallen on the way before he graduated and did his PhD, he is generally very sympathetic. He says, "Yes, I did this same thing, you know, I also made this same mistake of making 4+2=5. My son, it is not like that, do it this way." So you see, the failures are always more sympathetic, more loving, more compassionate, because they have needed that love and sympathy and compassion themselves, and know the value of that love and sympathy and compassion.

God, unfortunately, or fortunately, for us, has no mind. This is the great teaching of my Master. God cannot possibly have a mind because, if there is a mind, there is consciousness. If there is consciousness, there is consciousness of good and bad, of life and death, of myself and yourself. And the duality of existence takes birth in his mind and He ceases to be God at the instant He is born. So Babuji's greatest research, I would say, is this finding that God cannot possibly have a mind. Therefore, He cannot even know He is God. How can He, therefore, answer your prayers, you see, coming back to the question of prayer. Which God? Where? How will He recognize that He is being addressed? "Oh God!" I shout in the wilderness you know. Yes, but who is to listen to me? Therefore, you know, in His ultimate mercy, compassion, He sends Himself in another way. You see how it is done! It is a miracle, it is a mystery.

Perhaps, as Babuji once told me when I asked him, "How does this happen?", he said, "You will know it on the day you achieve that state yourself." It is like parentage for children, you see. A little girl wants to know how children are born. When she gets married she knows by personal immediate experience. She does not have to be told anything, you know. What is love? Well, when you fall in love with someone you know. Isn't it? What is a plum? For an Indian who has never eaten one, well, you eat it and you know. Isn't it?

So this is the value of direct perception, personal experience, which is the only recognized form of knowledge in Vedic science. No doubt we have books, but the books were written by those who had this direct personal experience of the Ultimate. They did not theorize, they did not philosophize. They wrote out of their personal experience. Now the wise should seek that personal experience, not that knowledge which has come out of that experience. Unfortunately that is the tendency, to read what they have written, not to do what they did and to become what they became.

Therefore, coming back to prayer once again, you know, I go wandering here and there a bit. Coming back to prayer again, Master said, "If you pray to God, I mean I have no objection, how will such a God answer you when he has no mind, no consciousness, no sense perception? Therefore, pray to the Master." And when we pray to the Master, even this element of begging perhaps sometimes, you know, he condones. Because of his sympathy — he is a human being — he says, "This guy has come to me in his suffering, in his anxiety, I have to do something." So when we pray we do not draw upon the goodness of the Master, we draw upon the love of the Master, and the sympathy and the compassion which flows with that love. Therefore, he is able to assist us, whatever, however stupid our request may be.

So prayer to the Master has some meaning, though I personally have said, several times, that to me that also is a little

The Role of the Master

obnoxious. Because when we claim he is divinity in human form, he is the all-knower, the all-wise, the love personified, to pray and to remind him, "Babuji my son is sick," or "My wife is sick," or "My business is failing," seems to question his divinity a little, you see. Of course I can understand that in our misery of the moment we have only him to fall back upon, and therefore we do it. Every one of us does it and I do not think, at that moment, it is wrong. Because, if I knew it was wrong, I would not do it. But in that moment of terror in the middle of the night, somebody is dying, there is the death rattle in the throat, and you do not know what to do, you pray to the Master.

And very often, most often, the miracle occurs that something happens and a person who is literally dead is taken up again. Let it not be thought that Lazarus was the only instance of a dead person being raised by a superior being. It is happening again and again. I mean, it is like these books of the existence after death that we read. It can be written only by one who has had that experience. So the true testament to such experience is the one who has undergone it, and I know there are several in our Mission whom Babuji has thus blessed, not with just gifts of happiness and joy and health but with life itself. That is why a Master is life-giver, you see. And a life-giver can be none but God Himself. So, I am trying to come to the divinity of the Master in the sort of invertendo form. You see, the logic of it? So to pray to such a one, well, that is why the prayer is addressed to, 'O Master!'

So why should we pray? You know, very often abhyasis ask, new people ask, "You too have a prayer like Christianity? Oh, I do not want prayer. I do not want a system which has a prayer." They do not know what they are losing. So it is the duty of preceptors to understand what is prayer, why it is advocated in Sahaj Marg, and explain this. Because, otherwise it is like, you know, for a small black spot on the moon, I would not see the full moon at all. "Oh, it is blemished!" So this is why I have gone rather into length on prayer.

Then we come to meditation. Meditation has been defined as thinking constantly about something. Rest, you all know why we meditate. But please remember that meditation is only a technique. It is not an end in itself. And this is exemplified by the often repeated fact that many people just go into meditation and start snoring and they are not aware of anything else. It is done in a mechanical way. And they enjoy the meditation rather than do the meditation. And Babuji used to say, "This is a mechanical thing and they have no progress at all." Because when we meditate, it has to be a dynamic process in which the goal is always in our view. That is, a movement towards the goal is involved. Otherwise it is like sitting in a static train. Even a TGV, you know, if it is drawn up in the yards of the Paris stations, and is destined to go only tomorrow morning, if I sit in it, it is not going to take me anywhere. It must move.

So meditation is a process, it is not an end in itself. I say this because I find often preceptors say, "Meditate and everything is solved." Nothing is solved by meditation. By meditation, we meditate. What do we achieve by meditation? Then if people ask, you see, by mastering the ability to think continuously of something, I gain a regulatory control over my own mind. I have now the possibility of applying that mind where I choose. It is able to reveal to me the truth of whatever I seek. So at its peak, meditation can do nothing but serve as an instrument of revelation, because the mind is perfected, the mind is regulated, and the mind becomes one-pointed and now I can use it for everything except to know God. Because God, not being an object, cannot be the object of concentration. Therefore, no concentration can ever reveal the presence of God, notwithstanding that even yoga abhyas, yogic science says 'concentrate', it is a misnomer. Unfortunately, in the

The Role of the Master

English language it has been, I think, mis-translated to mean concentration. Concentration can do nothing but reveal that which is, in its true colours.

Constant remembrance — what for? Because meditation is very clearly defined in its scope, in its function. Meditation, by itself, cannot take me anywhere. It can only give me a mind which is in my control, an absolute mind. Now comes the role of constant remembrance, because Babuji has said, "If you are able to remember the Master continuously, constantly, the need for meditation drops off." Why? Here is the great difference between most of the yogic systems and ours. Because here the foundation of a spiritual association with the Master is love. And to create love there is no other way but constant remembrance. Babuji has said, I mean all of you know it, again and again we have spoken about it, that we remember that which we love. Therefore, if you want to love something, reverse the process and remember it. By remembrance we learn to love that which we remember. And, therefore, when love begins to grow in the heart of the abhyasi for the Master, remembrance also in a way ceases. I would not say remembrance ceases, it ceases as an activity. Remembrance now is very much of an activity! We **try** to remember. As people say, "I remember him often every day," you see. And as one American boy put it, "I practice constant remembrance several times a day." It is an effort at the moment, you see, remembrance is an effort. But when we are perfect in it, Babuji once told me, "If an abhyasi can practice constant remembrance for just one week, he cannot stop remembering after that." Because it becomes the sort of, the riverbed on which the river of consciousness itself flows. It becomes the substratum of our existence, as an act of remembrance, as an effort. So we have to bring this remembrance to the subconscious level where it becomes the foundation on which every existence was built. And then when that love is

Courmettes

perfected for the Master, as Babuji said, "When your love is strong enough to knock on the door of His heart, and He condescends to open the door and see who is there, and He sees you, your job is over." So, constant remembrance is also a practice, is also a step. It has no meaning in itself, it has no efficacy in itself, except to lead to a condition where we love the Master totally, continuously.

So prayer, meditation, constant remembrance. I think that finishes the list which I had not tackled yesterday. And now perhaps we have to come to today's topic [he chuckles] rather tardily I am afraid. What is the topic for today? Yes! One thing I have left out, very important, cleaning!

Now cleaning. It is a very obvious thing we all know. As I have said so many times, if I have stored gasoline in a bottle and I wish to buy milk in it, I have to clean it first. So when we are trying to put something into us which is of the highest order of existence, the divine essence of the Master by way of his transmission, we have to make ourselves fit to receive it. That is the cleaning process.

So the preceptor's work in cleaning is a very vital component of the spiritual work of the Master. Let us not belittle it to ourselves by saying, "Oh it is only cleaning, you know, I am not a sweeper!" Remember with how much love you used to prepare Babuji's house before he arrived in Denmark. Days and days given to washing and cleaning and painting, redecorating, putting candles on the steps, giant candles by the door. Beautiful new bedspreads, carpet, costing, I do not know, 50,000 kroner, and to serve as a jumbo ashtray that big glass tray with the brass rim. A jumbo ashtray, because the hookah used to be positioned in the centre of it to protect the carpet. How much love you lavished, how much money you spent, how much time you devoted to the purification of a mere house

The Role of the Master

for His presence, where he was going to stay a few days and then leave. How much more time you should devote to this house where he is going to be eternally present?

As I said in one of my talks last year, that the physical living Master is ours for a few years — no more. You see, we have that unfortunate tragic experience in our own lives. All of us felt we had the Master forever and now feel we have lost him. Both are wrong. We never had him forever because that forever was a physical forever which was stupid. The feeling that we have lost him is even more stupid, because how can you lose a Master who is eternal? This feeling comes because of that fact, I spoke, I think, in Chatenay-Malabry, the only talk I gave in 1982, that unless you bring the Master into your heart, in His spiritual essence, which is carried through from life to life, if he does not leave you behind, you are going to leave him behind. You know, it is like a parting at a railway station, whether you are in the train and your lover is on the platform, or whether your lover is in the train and you are on the platform, the parting is equally, what shall I say, sad, miserable. So who goes first, who goes last?

I said this because at that time many young people asked me, "Chari what will we do when the Master is dead?" I mean a very crude question, but nevertheless a question which showed their anxiety for their future. What would they do if they are left orphans on the spiritual field? So I told them then in that talk, "My dear friend, this question everyone is asking. What would you do if you died first?" I mean, many people have died before the Master. What would you do?

Therefore, the imperative need, you see, to carry him in your heart in his spiritual form, from which he can never leave you, from which you can never be parted because it is yours through eternity. Therefore, when such a miraculous possibility exists and we in our sadhana have made the heart so pure that we do not have to inform him, he comes himself. He says, "Ha, ha! That is my residence, there I go." Nothing can stop him you see. And once he is there who can remove him? He is not a tenant who does not pay his rent and you can go to the court and evict him. He is the Master of that residence, and all that you have done is to have purified the place of the Master and invited him in. He has accepted and he has taken up residence permanently, eternally.

Babuji has always said, which was a great satisfying thing to me, he said, "From my preceptors I expect work, not results." Very canny old man he was, you see, because when you work the results must be there. But when he made this statement, "I do not expect results from you," it relieves us of a tremendous burden of responsibility which we stupidly impose on ourselves thinking that we are responsible for the result of the work. It shows an ignorance of the principle of surrender. When I surrender, it means I surrender the result of my work to him. It is his. I work. What he wants, he will establish. You see, it is like a Master who says, "Build a house." Then he says, "No, no, you know, I want this door knocked out and put here." The builder cannot say, "I spent twenty-four hours on building this door." "Okay, I am paying for it." So you see, at one stroke, this statement by the Master, that I want your work not your result, relieves us of ninety-nine percent of our problems. Because most of us, when we sit down, we are worried about the result. When we are worried about the result, we weaken our mind, we weaken our will, *ipso facto* inevitably our work is going to fail. I mean, Master or no Master, we are failures because of our own expectation of failure when we start the work. Therefore, it is necessary to sit with absolute confidence. And how can this confidence be built up? Well, if you have it already, very good. If not, the technique that my Master taught

The Role of the Master

to me, "Think the Master is sitting there. If necessary imagine his beard on your face and the problem is solved, now it is not you, he is sitting there."

So you see, all this is very important for cleaning, for ourselves, for the abhyasis, to be faithful to the Master in our performance of the duty we have voluntarily accepted from him, to be faithful to the abhyasis whom we have taken responsibility for, who come to us with tremendous longing, yearning, faith in us.

You see, this is the most terribly responsible job a person can have. All the rest, you know, people come and say, "Oh, I could not get a holiday because I have a conference to attend." You feel responsible for conferences and seminars which any other stupid fellow earning your salary could do. A teller in a bank says, "I cannot leave my counter." Why not? Counting dollar notes, any fool can do it. Though you are highly paid for it, it does not mean it is an important job, you see. But this job which is vital to their existence, the thousands we have accepted, to ourselves, we do not understand its importance, we do not understand its vital significance in our existence, that it is not for today, it is for the immensity of the future which we call eternity. If only we would understand its significance there would not be these foolish excuses, you see, "I can attend for two days; my wife is troubling me; my son is sick." So what? If you believe in the Master do not you think he would look after your wife, change her attitude, look after your son who is sick?

And when the Master came to you for three months in 1972 at the age of seventy-three, did you ask him, "Babuji, your sons are there, your fields are there, your house is there, who is going to look after them in your absence?" Did you ask him? "No, no, Babuji, please stay one more week." So why this dual approach? You know, one for ourselves, and one for the Master. What is sauce for the goose is sauce for the gander. If he can leave his family and his home and his farm and his estate and his work, and come to you for three months, cannot you go to him for three days when he is there? Or six days which he wants?

So you see, all this is the need of the hour, to awaken within ourselves the truth of what we are doing, the vitalness of what we are doing, why we are doing it. Why are we here? What on earth are we doing this meditation for? Why am I associated with a master? What for? Because something in us tells us that without this we cannot exist. At the same time, we think it is bread and honey and, you know, *baguette* and *fromage* which keeps us alive. This is the duality of our misconceptions. "All this, and heaven too!" And, as I said in one of my first talks in 1972, "You want heaven and all this too?" When we believe, as Christ said, that not a sparrow shall fall, you know, all those stories: the two loaves and the five fishes which fed the multitude. Well, if he could do it once, he could do it eternally, always, for everybody. But we trot out these stories, you know, as a proof of our faith in the Almighty or the Christian tradition. And when it is applied to ourselves we say, "No, no, you see, today if I do not go to work, I will lose my job." Where is your Christ now? Or where is your Master now?

So you see, we should not have this flippantly dual attitude that, I am an abhyasi **and** this, I am a preceptor **and** this. **I am a preceptor!** I also have to do something to earn my living, the minimum necessary, you see. Spiritual law says, "Yes, you have to exist, you have to eat, you have to do it by your own labour." But how much? Now if a man is earning, let us say, $80,000 in the US, it is a fat lot of money, you know, by any standards. And when they are hankering for more money, more promotion and they are giving their life to that job, from eight

The Role of the Master

hours to ten hours, to twelve hours, to fourteen hours, and neglecting a half hour meditation and a ten minute cleaning, are they stupid or are they wise? And when they die, where are they going to leave all these $80,000 multiplied by so many years, minus what they have spent? Where are they going to leave it? Are they going to take it with them?

So spiritual science says, this is all your stomach, you know, one span out of seven and one half, less than fourteen percent. That much time of the day, if you give to it is enough, fourteen percent of twenty-four hours is all that you need to earn your living, if you do it rightly. I mean every farmer does it. You see the poor people on the streets, they do it. They are not dead; though by your standards they are as good as dead. But they say, "Look at me, I have no responsibility, you know. I have my food, I sleep on the pavement, I am happy, I have no house to lock up, no wife to protect, no children to send to school. Look at these rich people, you know, they come in a car, they have to lock the expensive thing. They have to take their briefcase with them. When they carry the briefcase, they have to hold it close to themselves, so that somebody does not pull it away. The wife wears a necklace round her neck, which is worth a couple of hundred thousands and she has to wear the sari over it so that nobody pulls it away. Why wear a necklace which you are going to cover up? [laughter] And why millions of dollars worth of jewelry in bank vaults, you see, and wearing artificial jewels to a birthday party or a wedding?" And they are right, you see. How right they are, we do not know. Because in our misery, we seek protection from that wealth. "Oh, I have seven million in the bank, Chari, I can never be in trouble." And along comes a nice tidal wave, Mary III, which sweeps the coast and your three million dollars is gone. And you are worse than a beggar because he knows how to exist from day to day, you do not. See, this is the misery of richness, and the beauty and, shall we say, sublimity of poverty, if you would only like to go a little beyond the skin depth of appearance.

So why faith in the Master? For this reason you see: that by meditation I clear this instrument of my perception, "The ultimate instrument," as Babuji said, "for your destruction and for your elevation." Nothing can destroy you so totally as your mind if it goes wrong, nothing can serve to raise you to divinity as your mind can. Therefore, in the raja yoga technique, it is the mind that we use, it is the mind that we master, it is the mind that we apply. But having done that, the entire thing is transferred to the heart. As we say in yogic psychological terminology: the heart now becomes the mind. We think with the heart, we see with the heart, we hear with the heart, we speak with the heart, the heart becomes **me**. And that is why in our, shall we say, native latent human wisdom, we always categorize a person by his or her heart: cold-hearted, warm-hearted, cruel-hearted, stone-hearted, iron-hearted, soft-hearted. You do not say, "He is a soft-brained fellow." It means something else, you see. [laughter] Soft-hearted, yes; soft-brained, no. It is the heart by which we describe a person. "What a lovely heart!" Even a lover you call a sweetheart, you see. Though you do not chew it up. [laughter]

That is the miracle of spirituality you see, that we make the entire existence by regulating the mind, by gaining the absolute control or regulation of the mind. We are now able to recognize the wisdom of having to transfer the entire cognitive, perceptive apparatus into the heart. Then begins true spirituality.

So I think perhaps you are all a bit tired. Not yet? So that is cleaning. [he chuckles] Now I think I should take up today's work. [laughter] Role of the Master, I have covered, you see.

The Role of the Master

If you put it in one word, the role of the Master is **total**, is **absolute**.

For one who is dabbling in spirituality, we have several masters. For a man it is the wife. The first master of a male is the wife. I mean all married men will agree to this. [laughter] Unmarried men stupidly imagine it to be otherwise, and they find out when it is too late. [he chuckles] [laughter] But then we have other masters, you know, the master in the office, the master here, the money-lender who is plaguing you for the return of his money. They are all our bosses, our masters. But the spiritual master has an absolutely total role. You cannot say that anything is exempt from him, or out of the purview of his regulation of your existence. As Babuji says, and used to say very often, "I cannot even breathe without Lalaji's permission. I cannot even drink a glass of water without his permission." That is the extent, or shall we say, the completeness of the totality of the Master's all-embracing purpose in our existence. But unfortunately, you know, till we come to a state of enlightenment perhaps, wisdom, we think a master is only for meditation, for cleaning and occasionally to answer our phone calls when somebody is desperately ill. But that is a very, I would not say it is wrong, but it is a limiting way of looking at the Master, because he can only respond in the way in which we accept him. When we fragment him, and accept him partially, he can only respond partially. When we accept him totally, his responsibility for us becomes total. This is why surrender epitomizes the absolute acceptance of the Master. Then, because we are totally his, he is totally ours, he looks after us totally, every aspect of our existence becomes his responsibility and we can live in that sublime innocence where we are desire-free, where we are fear-free, where we are even need-free because he is looking after us.

So, how to achieve that state? There again, the miracle is only by love we can surrender, not by fear. Of course, in the armies we surrender, to a thief on the streets we surrender our belongings. But between two human beings surrender is an act of love, not fear, not temptation. So if there is a failure, by and large, in human beings to surrender, it is because of, again let me say, religion's misuse of the powers vested in it to tempt and to threaten: fear of hell, temptation for redemption, for heaven. There was no evocation of the love principle in the heart of the devotee. Such stray cases as evolved into love, it was more their effort than the church's effort or the temple's effort.

So the role of the Master must be absolute if we are to benefit. Of course, if you think it is enough to go and sit before him and have a sitting once in a way, it is as good as going to the dentist once in six months, or to the bank once every Saturday to draw your money for the next week. No more than that. And now perhaps some of you understand it, I hope most of you understand it, and I wish all of you will understand this. Because, for your existence, it is enormously important that you know the role the Master plays in your life. Even more is it necessary for you to tell the abhyasis who come to you, what is the role that the Master has to play in their lives.

Therefore, Babuji said in that famous sentence in Munich, "Attach your heart with that of the Master and your mind with that of the preceptor." Preceptor is a guide, you see. Listen to him, obey him, practise what he tells you to practise, but love the Master. And, you know, he was such a shy man, my Master, who could never talk about himself, who could never ask for anybody's love. I mean, I have never seen him asking for anything. And for him to make such a statement showed the enormity of the ignorance prevailing among abhyasis, preceptors alike, which had to prod him into making this statement,

The Role of the Master

you see, "Give your heart to the Master and your mind to the preceptor." What torment must have been in his heart, you see, not that he was not loved; why should the Divine be loved, you see? It is a stupid thing that Divinity should ask for anything from any of us, but for the enormity of the loss that it was occasioning to the abhyasis who were being misguided by preceptors, who in their, perhaps, pride, arrogance or their need to be loved, diverted the abhyasis toward themselves rather than toward the Master. Now, this is a direct implication, a direct result out of this conviction, that the Master's role is absolute, not the preceptor's.

Now we have to remember a very important thing. Babuji told me very early in my life, "Remember, a preceptor serves the Master." We do not serve abhyasis. Very often we find, you know, when an abhyasi comes and says, "Oh, I am very happy, Mr. So-and-so, you have served me so much," And we say, "Yes, yes, I have done what is possible," — we slip one level. Because if the Master says, "No more transmission," we have to stop. If we do not stop, he will stop it himself. Because the main switch is there. Therefore, we serve the Master. He says, "Take up this person and give him sittings," we do it. If he says, "No, this person is not for you," we stop.

This is especially essential in the Western, Occidental society to understand, where, if you will permit me to say so, you have these funny conceptions of compassion. "Oh, this poor man, he has got cancer, why should I not take him and give him some cleaning?" No. You have been given a specific job. Do it! See, it is like a carpenter and a mason and an electrician working on a house. The electrician sees something wrong going on, or maybe he thinks it is wrong, you see, and he wants to do the carpenter's job. The boss comes and says, "You do your job, my friend, this is not your job." "No, no, but this is your house he is ruining." "Well, that is my look-out."

Courmettes

"When I am here to look after the cancers and the, whatever it is, AIDS, and leukemias, and what not, why do you bother about it?" You see, if the Master had the normal arrogance of the human being, the pride in his position and the need to protect himself, he would say it. He would say, "Look after your work, these are your abhyasis, you transmit to them, clean them, make them evolve. Why are you worried about him and her and that?" This is very necessary, you see, because in the West, though we revile Christianity, we have attached ourselves to this concept of compassion in a very wrong way. Compassion is for Him, not for us. I told you a few days ago when you read, "Vengeance is mine, saith the Lord," compassion is also His. We are servants, we obey, you see. He says, "Do this," we do it. He says, "Today you sleep," I sleep.

People in Denmark will remember, occasionally I used to be overworked and Babuji said, "Today, you sleep, no work." And I said, "Twenty-three people I have to give sittings to tomorrow." He said, "That is not your concern. You are overburdened, your brain is taxed, go to sleep." And I slept, very happy to sleep. [laughter] I mean, that is what we are there for. We are there to obey, you see. It is most important to remember that preceptors serve the Master, not humanity. **He** serves humanity, **we** serve the Master. And in serving him, we work on humanity for him, in obedience to his orders, to fulfil his purpose in life. So the Master's role is that total, you see, that he can say yes or no to life and death, yes or no to existence or non-existence, yes or no to health or sickness, to wealth or poverty, to absolutely anything.

Once I asked him, "Is there anything you cannot do?" He laughed and kept quiet. He did not say no; nor did he say yes, he laughed. Three days later, I tackled him. I said, "Babuji, is there something you cannot do?" He said, "If Lalaji wishes, there is nothing I cannot do." But there also you see the Master

The Role of the Master

has to permit. Even the Master has his Master. He is the regulatory control to see that this man does not become arrogant, proud, power-mad, power-crazy as we say, and says, "I can do anything I choose." So that is the safety valve which Nature creates even in the line of Masters, that if something should go wrong here, the fuse closes.

Therefore, you see, we have to be very conscious, always alert. What are we doing? Why are we working? For whom are we working? Whom are we really serving? And remember this, as I said, this is, I do not know, the eleventh or twelfth time, "His role in our existence is total." If you want anything, seek from him. Prayer — pray to him. Ask — ask him, not anybody else.

Then, the purpose of the Mission, the efficacy of the method. Efficacy of the method I do not have to speak specially about, you all know it, you have all felt its efficacy in yourselves. It is our duty to prove the efficacy of the system first in ourselves and then in the abhyasis who come to us. What has worked upon me must work upon another person, given the same co-operation that I could give to my Master. I mean, people talk of science and reproducibility of results. What can be more reproducible than a Master creating a Master? Isn't it? In management schools, well, they create managers but they do not create bosses; but here you create the boss himself. As Babuji said, "I do not make slaves, I make Masters." So, it is our duty to prove the system's ability and its capacity, as abhyasis upon ourselves, as preceptors upon the abhyasis who come to us, and that is how the efficacy of the system is transmitted down the line, as it were. So it is a double duty we have, again. Because if we are inefficient, if we fail, it is the Master's failure. Nobody is going to say, "You failed or she failed." They say, "What is the system, what is the Ram Chandraji you are talking so much about? Nothing has happened." It is his name, it is his reputation, it is the Mission's fair name that is always at stake. So remember, we do not work for ourselves, we work for the Master. The Mission is His, the method is His, He created it, our successes are His, our failures are always ours. Therefore the need, even for this seminar, that we should try to improve our capacities, our efficacies, our efficiency, not by repeatedly doing what we do in the material world. A carpenter becomes good by repeatedly carpentering whatever he has to carpenter. But here, it is by increasing our awareness, making it as near total as we can, ridding ourselves of fear, of nervousness, of commitment to results.

Excuse me, this is a very important thing to recognize. In the West immediately they will say, "Oh, no commitment to result? Thank you, I am going. I will find another system. Goodbye." Such a person does not deserve to be here. We are not committed to results because the result is guaranteed by Him whom we serve, provided you do what you have to do. So you see, the efficacy of the system is total. As the Master's role in our existence is total, the efficacy of the system is total. It is our failure which makes it less than successful or less than perfect, and it is never his fault.

What is the Mission for? Now this is something you know, when we were talking of prayer in 1972, there was a lot of, you know, brou-ha-ha about Mission. Why Mission? It smacks of Christianity. So if you call something by a name which you do not like, you do not like the thing itself! So Babuji said, "What can I do?" Of course, he had his own inimitable way of answering questions. I remember it was in the preceptors' meeting in Morges, in Switzerland, Mr. Poray raised this question, repeatedly he raised this question of the Mission, you see. Babuji said, "Look, I am telling you, I also do not like it. But I am called Ram Chandra. I must be Ram Chandra in Germany, Ram Chandra in Finland, Ram Chandra in India.

The Role of the Master

Suppose I have a different name in each country, how will you recognize me? So since it has been given this name in honour of my Master, I cannot now change it." You know he just very adroitly sidetracked the issue. Then everybody had to agree.

But we have these deep-seated prejudices against things and names and places which are totally irrational. I mean prejudice *per se* is irrational. So whenever we talk of the Mission, people say, "What is this Mission, another Christianity? You know they are not only calling it a mission, they have the prayer, they have a Master and you must pay money." Now this money is a big bugbear. We are willing to pay for *baguettes* and for all the silly things: *Asterix*, thirty-six francs. It does not bother us. But when we talk of an ashram and the need to have an ashram, not for the Master, the Master is not going to take away your ashram from here, you see, or from wherever it may be. Even the Shahjahanpur ashram still exists in Shahjahanpur, though the Master is physically no more there. There is this deep-seated fear, you know, that when you give, you are selling yourself. I would have thought that when you are receiving you are selling yourself. Isn't it? It is receiving which makes us obliged to the giver. How can giving make you obliged? So please try to accept a right understanding of what a mission is. A mission is a name, it is nothing more, you could call it Shri Ram Chandra Institute. Or you could call it *Maison de Ram Chandra*. What does it matter? A rose by any other name has the same number of thorns! Isn't it? Can you find a rose without thorns? That it smells as sweet by any other name, that we leave to the poets and to the artists. I am concerned with the reality of the situation. When I reach out for a rose, I get scratches on my hand. How to avoid it? You cannot break off the thorns and then pluck the rose. We accept it as it is, you see.

Now when we talk of a mission, this instinctive revulsion, revolt against the word 'mission', you should kindly remove from your minds, it can be done by cleaning — one technique. The better thing is to accept that it is only a name. What does it matter if Sigismund Leiber is called Sigismund Niebel or Helmut Peiper? It does not matter as long as the man is the same. I mean, Helmut Peiper could also be called Sigismund Niebel for all I care. [he chuckles] What I mean is, it is the person who is valuable, not his name. So what is the Mission doing? The Mission is an organization. Why do we need an organization? Precisely to harness the efforts of the Master for humanity. You see, if it was one Master serving one disciple, we do not need anything. They could have a walking stick, the Master holding one end of it, the disciple holding the other end of it and walking free wherever they go, being fed, they can sit and transmit under a tree and he reaches his illumination and both go into, I do not know, *mahasamadhi* there itself. The job is over.

But when you have to build an institution where you have to take whatever you are offering to the people, not like a temple or a church where you invite the people to come to you, you need an organization. And what is the organization for? It is for your benefit. What does a master want with the Mission? Nothing! He had his Master who did not have a mission. But, "Why does my Master want a mission?" you could ask then. Precisely because my Master's Master probably trained 250 people in his lifetime in a geographical area not exceeding a diameter of twenty-five miles, or a hundred miles, from where he stayed. That was all. I mean, when I say this it is not any discredit to Lalaji, and I am not trying to degrade the work that he did. His work was immense; but he is the man who planted the seed, you see. It is easy for somebody to sow a seed and walk away, "I have done my work, I do not need an organization. What for? Chari, all that you need is a hole in the ground, put the seed and cover it up." Yes. When the plant comes who

The Role of the Master

is going to look after it? Now you need shears for pruning it, something to dig around its roots, something to water it with, insecticides to keep it free of termites and what not. The need comes **after** the seed is sown. So you see, one man sowed the seed; then the tree has to be looked after, or the trees have to be looked after by another man. Then comes the role of the harvester, you know, who has to go mango by mango by mango. And this problem is solved beautifully by American technology. You have harvesters, you see, they can even pluck bunches of grapes. So organization only reflects the growth of an institution.

In the days when Europe had no cars, and people were wandering on their feet, you had no traffic rules, no green and red lights, no policemen. You could walk as you choose, left side, right side. What did it matter if you bumped into another human being? Nobody was killed. But when you have cars of six hundred horsepower, and hundreds of thousands of them on the roads, obviously you need discipline, you need an organization, you need electricity, you need lights, you need a powerhouse, you need tax revenues. How is it going to run without **your** contributing to it? To every red light on the street, you have paid somewhere, sometime, you know, something. For the roads, you have paid. Why are you paying the tolls: twelve francs, two francs, seventeen francs, twenty-eight francs? And you pay with such abandon, you know. "It is nothing, you see, *une bagatelle.*" By the time you go from here to Marseille, you know you pay something like forty francs. It is no joke. And you think nothing of it. But when you say, buy a book, "Oh, but you know, Chari, Sahaj Marg — we should not ask for money." Yes, we are not asking for money, we are selling you a book! Isn't it? Are you giving your money free for something which is not given back to you? So please remember, the organization exists for you; books are printed for you; if the Master travels, he travels for you; if there is going to be an ashram, it is for you.

The Master, he can live under a tree, you see. Do not think only you Europeans can live in tents; the Indians are famous for living without tents. And not only in this semi-cold of your Pyrenees and your little hills, but in the Himalayas. You do not know such mountains in Europe. So do not belittle the Indian when he asks you for something. "Oh, this man wants bread and butter." Well, give him a glass of water if you cannot afford the bread and butter, but do not say he asks for something. He never asks. My Master never asked for anything. When the Shahjahanpur ashram was proposed, he was extremely reluctant to have an ashram, because he knew the attitude of the abhyasis. Those who never give are the biggest protesters, because they want to justify their non-giving. The one who gives quietly puts the money somewhere and walks away. He does not want it to be known; he is shy of his charity. "Let not thy right hand know what thy left hand has done." But the one who is not giving, he is raising both his arms up in protest. "Why should I give, why does Sahaj Marg ask for money?" you know. And in that act, in that desperate shout, he exposes the emptiness of his hands, and, unfortunately, the emptiness of his heart.

Now I want preceptors to be totally committed to this concept: that an organization is essential, that it has to exist, that it has to be supported. Because I know there are preceptors even here who have rebelled at the idea of collecting money for this or that or whatever. Preceptors have to be committed to the purpose of the Mission, which is the purpose of the Master, which is not any ordinary process of charitable deeds or social uplift. It is evolutionary uplift of humanity itself. It is a task of unimaginable scope that my Master has undertaken. And if you belittle it, you belittle evolution itself, you belittle

The Role of the Master

God Himself. So that is all I have to say about the Mission. Please remember, because from **your** conviction alone can come conviction when you speak to others. We do not speak because we are wise. I mean, a really wise man knows that what he transmits is confidence, conviction, which he has earned out of his own personal experience of the path. Wisdom you can get from books, from dictionaries. Conviction must come from inner conviction; strength must come from inner strength; confidence must come from inner confidence. These things, unless **we** have we cannot give them to others.

Therefore I pray, you see, that all of you should get right understanding of the system, of the Master, of what we are doing. We are doing nothing less than endeavoring to upgrade humanity to the level of the angels and gods and beyond. It is not an ordinary task, it is not even a super-human task. It is a **divine** task in which you are involved. Please understand it and work accordingly.

Thank you.

4

Stages of Spiritual Progress

Courmettes, France
Tuesday, July 12, 1988

So, today we start speaking about the *yatra* and the three major regions, spiritual regions, the heart, the mind and the central region. Somebody has asked for an exact definition of what is a *yatra*.

Yatra is a Sanskrit word meaning a journey, a travel. So any journey is a *yatra*. In India it is very common to say, "I am going on a *yatra*." If it is, for instance, for a religious purpose, a pilgrimage, we call it *tirth yatra*. You see, each religious or holy place is called a *tirth*. What you call a watering place, at least, you know, where you drink the waters.

So that used to be the idea of a *yatra*. And then in spirituality we have the inner journey of the self, whether it is a real journey or not, I do not know, but it is there, and therefore in the Sanskrit language the spiritual journey is called a spiritual *yatra*. So this *yatra*, unless it begins there is no progress, you see. At the first, I mean, at the commencement itself I should like to clarify one concept. There is something which is a sort of a horizontal expansion, you see, and there is vertical growth. There are two things. Like you can swim on the surface of an ocean, round and round in a spiral path, and keep on going, but you are still on the surface of the ocean. You are not going up, you are not going down. And if you want pearls you dive thirty, forty, fifty, a hundred feet. That is about all you have to do, you see.

And now it is this vertical growth which really matters. Obviously! You see, when flying was started, if you remember the Wright brothers, the first plane, or whatever they called it, probably hopped into the air and skipped back again onto the ground, a matter of a few feet. What distinguished it from other craft was that it took off from the ground. It does not matter whether you fly one foot above the ground or one hundred thousand feet above the ground, you are still in a different dimension. And at whatever speed you may, sort of, cruise on the ground, even those famous racing cars which do four hundred, five hundred miles per hour on the Utah flats, they are still in a different dimension from a plane, a DC-3 for instance, which may do only a hundred miles an hour. It is the **dimension** which makes the difference, not the speed. In spirituality we deal essentially with dimensions of growth. It is possible to expand infinitely in one dimension and not grow. Unfortunately, we are conditioned to think in terms of growth associating it in our minds with physical growth: bigger, biggest; smaller, smallest, things like that. Growth by accretion, or reduction by attrition is the prevalent idea. But in Sahaj Marg it is something swelling up like a balloon in all three dimensions at one time.

But in the spiritual practice, in sadhana, there is a state called the *avadhoota gati*. *Gati* only means a state; *avadhoota*, means that he is stuck, though he may be expanding in that area, you see. Many saints, so called, in India are of that *avadhoota* category, they are called *avadhootas*. They seem to be apparently developing. They have the ability to sing ecstatically the names of God, in praise of God, divine (or whatever you call it) chants. Then they start giving up things. They give up the wife, leave the house, give up their children, jobs, wandering around like mendicants. Then they start taking off their clothes, until they end up with virtually nothing. And you

Stages of Spiritual Progress

know, the not very well educated section of the population in India, which is a very large section of the population, ninety-six percent, they revere these people as *avadhootas*. They give them food, they offer them shelter, they give them, sometimes, even money to buy a *bidi*, for instance, you know the country cigarettes that they make with leaves. But the *avadhootas* do not go anywhere, you see. They are stuck in that one level, and they may become ecstatic, which is just perhaps a highly elevated emotional state, but has nothing to do with spirituality.

Ecstasy *per se* is not spiritual. There are many types of ecstasy; you have the ecstasy of eating, of drinking, and other things. In fact, in the *Vedas*, the most revered spiritual texts of India, **the** authority on all matters temporal, spiritual, ritualistic, where you have a mantra and a ritual prescribed for everything from prenatal to post mortem conditions, they govern your life with a rigidity which is unimaginable, and the priest is entering in every phase of your life. Before you are born, your mother has a purificatory ritual called a *seemanta*. Of course, it is naturally preceded by marriage. So starting from marriage, the mother, then the child, at birth it has a purificatory ritual. Then at the age of seven or eight, if it is a Brahmin child, it has to be invested with the sacred thread, which makes it 'twice born', once into this mortal world, once into the spiritual world. Then it goes on and on until you die, and then after death, your son has to perform so many things for you, you see.

In that *Veda*, in one of the *Upanishads*, it is called the *Taittiriya Upanishad*, a very famous *Upanishad*, there the disciple asks his guru, "What is this for which we are striving here, and how do we achieve it?" And the guru says, "By *tapas*." *Tapas* is what you call *askesis*. And then he goes on to describe the stages of *tapas*, how to achieve them. And at the end he comes to this famous statement that the Ultimate is bliss: *"anandam brahmeti vyajanat!"*

And the disciple asks, "What is *anandam*? How do you describe this bliss?" And strangely enough, the unit of human enjoyment, pleasure, ecstasy, the ultimate happiness that a human being can ever achieve is stated to be in sexual fulfilment. And the guru says, "Know that to be the unit of human enjoyment, human pleasure, beyond which the human being can aspire to nothing. That is the *sumum bonum* of human ecstasy." Then he goes on, you know, to multiply it a hundred times, that is what the *pitarloka*, in the fathers' world, you know, the world of the fore-fathers, they enjoy; multiply that by a hundred times, that is what the *devas* enjoy, not in terms of sex, but in terms of ecstasy, for there is no sex there. And ultimately, you come to the *Brahmanandam*, which is the bliss of *Brahma* himself, the creator, which is probably a million-fold the ecstasy that you have here from this ritual copulatory act. So you see, this sort of bliss is available through yogic techniques, without participation in a sex ritual, which is what these *avadhootas* achieve. And they go into ecstasy, they tear off their clothes, they tear their hair, dance in ecstasy, and people think they are great saints.

Master has warned, beware of such ecstasy because it is only a bloated ego enjoying a bloated ecstasy which is not real. So that is why I am saying, specifically in relation to the *yatra*, that the *avadhoota gati* is only a horizontal moment, however infinite it may be. One inch of vertical growth is far, far transcendental to millions of miles of horizontal travel. So the true *yatra* is the *yatra* of the soul from one region to the other by moving from one point to the next point, to the next, to the next, to the next, and so on.

Does the soul really move? Now that is a good question, you see. Whether it is a symbolism adopted for purposes of explaining, you see — when we have physical worlds separated by space and distance, we can think of motion taking us from somewhere to somewhere, and when that is also inevitably partaken, or participated in in time, in a frame of time, from some when to some then, you see. But where there is no space, where there is no time, is there really a motion either through space or time? Who is to answer this?

Nevertheless, the concept of *yatra* is important because it is possible for a preceptor to identify the soul in its location. Inevitably, at least in modern times, you cannot possibly find anybody other than at the first point. It is not possible. I say this with total conviction because Babuji told me he had only one case in his whole lifetime where he got one abhyasi who was already in the fourth point when he came to him. The only person who ever came to Babuji outside of the first point was this one single case in his entire lifetime. And Babuji said, "I gave him a sitting. I was astonished to see he was in the fourth point, and I was amazed at the amount of work he must have done to get there." I said, "Why? Four points, it is nothing much." This was in my days of what they call, you know, blissful ignorance [he laughs], when I thought everything is very easy, you see. Four points, what is the big joke, you see, what is the wonder about it? Then he told me the secret: that to move from the first point requires the power of the Master. You may never move from that point. Which is why this question of being born again and again and again and again, *ad infinitum, ad nauseum*, comes in.

So *yatra* may never take place, you see, except by the grace of the Master. And for those who undertake spiritual practice themselves thinking, in their enormous wisdom, that they can do it without the help of a guru — yes, perhaps they can reach this *avadhoota gati*, lull themselves into some sort of false security thinking they have made it, show some ecstasy by which they can show to the world that they have achieved something, and die a death which has inevitably to bring them back here again.

And what was this he told me about *yatra*? The *yatra* has to be begun by a master, and then, once the *yatra* begins, you see, he will permit us a little expansion within that centre, which we can also call a *yatra* within that centre, to answer the second question on that bit of paper. You can see actually the motion going around. And sometimes, when you are in the darkness, you can see some sparks of light, which have a circular motion. It is as if there is a spark here which is moving circularly in a clockwise manner. This, even that motion around that point, has to be stimulated by spiritual practice. That is possible by one's own effort, but it can take forty years, fifty years, a hundred years. With the grace of a master it can be in the very first sitting. It **can** be.

Now once this motion is set into being, or has been created, you see, you can say that now, for the first time, the soul is active. It has come out of that passive rigidity, that cold death where it was totally immobile, totally inconscient, into some sort of active participation. And that is why, I think, Lalaji has distinguished between *Brahman* and *atman*. *Brahman* is the Ultimate, the *atman* is the individual, embodied person's soul. He says, "This moves and grows, that thinks and grows," *At-man* and *Bruh-man*.

So without movement we cannot grow. This is established by this definition of the *atman*. That movement is *yatra*. And that movement has first to be stimulated within its centre, like a sick man when he is bedridden for twenty years, and by the grace of God, as they say, and by the help of the doctors, the first day he is able to hobble out of bed and go to the toilet. It is a day for rejoicing! "He is moving!" That is what we tell people, you know, telephone calls, "Yes, I am happy to tell you

Stages of Spiritual Progress

my dad is mobile again. He went to the toilet this morning." What a great achievement! We all do it every day, sometimes many times. But the beauty of that, the reassurance of those small, hobbling footsteps to the toilet assumes significance when we have been bedridden for twenty years, twenty-five years. And then, if you have a Master, with tears in your eyes you offer *prasad*. "Babuji, today by your grace, my father has moved to the toilet, may his **movement** continue."

So this is the importance of *yatra*, you see. That which has become motionless, ignorant, inconscient, sunk into itself in a mire of oblivion, it becomes active. Through activity, it gains. What does it gain? Not a thing, not a state, but its position on the evolutionary path, onto which it steps for the first time after who knows how many aeons of time of blissful ignorance. So, this is the importance of the *yatra*.

Now the Master permits expansion in that one point to a certain extent because he says, "I like that the soul gets a certain degree of command over that point. To the extent it is necessary, I allow it to grow within that point. Then I just give it a gentle push and put it on its way to the second point." Now the *yatra* between points, like it is **inter**-city and **intra**-city, you see, intermural, intramural; intercollegiate, intracollegiate. You have these terms, you know: within and in between two things of the same type. So there is a possibility of our expansion within a point which, if it is restricted to only there, can be infinite, taking infinite time, achieving no purpose whatsoever, taking you to the *avadhoota gati*. By the grace of the Master that can be stimulated by him, and you are allowed to achieve a certain degree of spiritual command over that point, then you are moved on to the next point. That is, now the **real** *yatra* of the soul is begun. When it comes to the second point, again he allows it to go around a bit to gain control, as he called it, command over that point, and then moves it on to the third.

Here comes the work of the preceptor. That when you clean the next point ahead, his work becomes easier to do. Just do like playing carrom [he makes a flicking motion with his finger], and it is pocketed.

Now, Babuji told me that in the old days this movement of the soul from the first point to the second point, once it has begun, used to take forty-five years under the most rigorous spiritual discipline, almost twenty-four hours a day, for the rishis in their caves in the jungles of the Himalayas. Forty-five years **after** the movement or *yatra* began within the point, which could take who knows how many years. Now if you understand that this is possible even within one sitting, you can understand and appreciate the enormous efficacy of the Sahaj Marg system. You will appreciate it even more when you hear that from the second point to the third point it took five times 45 years or 225 years. From the third to the fourth, five times 225 years or 1,125 years. From the fourth to the fifth, it took 5,625 years. From here [he points to point one] to here [he points to point six], 25,000 years. I just made up a computation once, and found that you need about 30,000 years to reach the point of liberation! So it is not surprising that few people have ever been liberated in the past. Who has 30,000 years of lifespan?

That is why Babuji was astonished when somebody came to him who was already in the fourth point. It is a minimum of 1,300 years of spiritual practice he must have devoted to himself, which means that during several past lives he had been at it, you know, with his nose to the grindstone! And the pity of it was, I mean Babuji almost had tears in his eyes, that person came once, he never came again. It would have taken perhaps just one more sitting to have given him his liberation, perhaps a few minutes of transmission. But that man never came again. I said, "Babuji, how is it possible that after spending 1,500

Stages of Spiritual Progress

years in these past existences and achieving a state at which you yourself wonder, how is it he did not come again?" He said, "That is the pull of the samskaras, the tendencies, you see." That is why his famous dictum, "Achieve it here, achieve it **now**." Do not say, "I will come back tomorrow. I have to go urgently today, I have my hair to cut or my grapes to pluck or my children to take to school."

If you miss this opportunity, it may never occur again. Tomorrow you may be reborn, yes, but you may not find a guru, you may not find a system, you may not find a school. Even Gurdjieff, whether charlatan or saint, nobody knows, he has warned, you see, "When you find a school stick with it, because if you lose it, even if it is next door, you may never find it again." I have told you that Babuji's neighbours did not know who he was, what he was. They only thought of him as an old man who had retired from court service, earning a few hundred rupees a month, venerable because of his age, respectable because he came from a rich family, but was himself poor, in a sense, yet, you know, not having the courage to deny him a salute when he walked past them.

So please remember the importance of cleaning, the importance of *yatra*. Without cleaning there is no *yatra*. It is not possible. Therefore the importance of the preceptor. People often ask, "Why preceptors? Cannot Babuji do it himself?" Of course he can. But to assist him in his work and to speed his work on the abhyasis, to make it possible for them to achieve their goal quicker, he uses preceptors to do what **we** might think of as the dirty work — cleaning! In a sense, it is dirty work. In a sense, it is very noble. You see, when you can prepare a person for liberation, it is by no means dirty. So, this is the importance of the *yatra*, and it must be correctly understood, because without a correct understanding and appreciation of the *yatra*, you are not going to understand the implications and the importance of cleaning, whether for yourself or for those who come to you. **Without cleaning, there is no *yatra*!** Write it in red ink!

Now, how does this work? I will draw the only graph or only sketch I am going to draw. You see there is one human, shall we say, characteristic that in the normal human being our tendencies are all outgoing, extrovert, and Babuji used to explain it to me with a diagram like this. I am not a good artist. The thought stream is supposed to come from the cosmic, you know, the *brahmanda mandal* point, from where everything originates, come down to the heart and take off from there in the outward direction. It is almost ninety-nine point nine percent recurring, this outward tendency. So that everybody, almost everybody, is extrovert. It is not to be wondered at, that is the tendency we have inherited, brought into this existence.

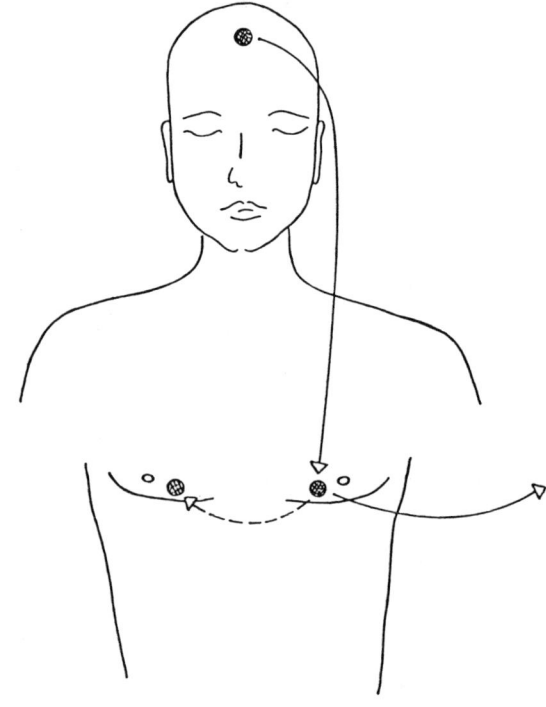

Stages of Spiritual Progress

The first job of the Master is to break it up into two streams and create as an inner diversion of at least one stream towards the second point, which is called the *atma chakra*. That is, the tendencies of the mind are given a turn inwards. He used to make a motion like this, as if you are turning a valve, twist it like this. It is necessary to leave quite a bit still going out, because otherwise we will lose interest in the external world. We have to live, we have to work, we have to earn money, we have to look after the children, raise the family. But turn as much as possible inwards, so that the pull of the soul can exert itself. This is called the *atma chakra*, the soul point. That is why we said yesterday that although the physical heart is on the left, the spiritual heart is on the right. And the tendencies when they are diverted or turned a little into this direction [pointing towards point two] now the *atma chakra* begins to exercise its pull towards itself.

It is like a magnet drawing the iron filings towards itself. Then begins in us this craving for our goal. If this is not done, nothing can happen, whatever you may do in meditation. So the first work of the Master is this. Now I asked him once, "Why do you leave this? [pointing to the outward flow] Why cannot you turn the whole thing?" He said, "He will become a vegetable. He will only think of God and lie there; even his milk and his food will have to be put into his mouth, he would be useless. It may be good for spirituality, but not as a human being."

So in the beginning, let us say, this is one third [pointing to the flow to point two] of the total, I mean, do not put it down as gospel truth, but two thirds outward tendency, one third inward tendency. Now what happens is, as we continue to meditate and we accept this pull of the soul towards itself, towards its real heart, we begin to be drawn more and more towards the internal spiritual life. And this thing [pointing to the outward flow] progressively fades away, almost until this is strong [pointing to the flow to point two] and this is weak [pointing to the outward flow]. You understand?

So, now what happens? I have very often felt that it is precisely when this stream of consciousness, tendencies stream, or the river of tendencies that flows down from here [pointing to point seven], through here, and to here, when it is diverted inside, most often that is the point at which abhyasis begin to rebel. In the sense that they say, "What is so hot about spirituality? You know, I am only twenty. I am only thirty. I am only sixty." The 'only' is always a prefix of the age. "I am only ninety." I have even heard a person say, "I am only ninety. I am not going to die. My doctor says everything is fine. Why don't you come back the day after tomorrow?" And the day after tomorrow, you go there, there is black crepe! Yes, the man is dead. You know, at that age you cannot say, the next moment, if you are going to be alive. I mean, at any age it is true.

So when this tendency is turned inwards, though the pull of the self towards itself is a very feeble, shall we say, almost unrecognizable pull, yet, to draw an analogy from the physical sciences, you know we have these major forces of gravitation and what they call the weak force and the strong force, the thing which binds the atom, the nucleus to its electrons is, I think, called a weak force. I am subject to correction. But its weakness is so strong that you need enormous power to break it apart. But it only acts within inter-atomic distances, that is of the order of millionths of centimetres, one millionths, half millionths. So you see, this works only within the space between, let us say, the nucleus and its surrounding electrons, whereas gravitation works over enormous distances, interstellar distances, intergalactic distances. Similarly this force which is very weak in the beginning yet has an inexorable, shall we say doggedness, about it, that once it gets hold of you, it will not let go. And of

Stages of Spiritual Progress

this we are afraid! So we want to run away at the first possible opportunity, and we seek all possible excuses to avoid spirituality altogether. And therefore, you see, we have this complaint from preceptors, "Oh, he took three sittings. He took four sittings. He came for three months and dropped out." It is very easily explained if you know the theory of the system. When this begins [pointing to the flow to point two], they run away. Why do they run away? Not because they do not know that this is desirable, but that is more desirable. It is not that I love Caesar less, but that I love Rome more! This is Rome [pointing outwards], this is Caesar [pointing to the heart], in this instant.

So we prefer to explore the beauties, the glamours, the ecstasies of the outer world, "After all, how much of existence do we have? Sixty years, Chari, eighty years." You see, in the other time it was, 'only sixty years.' "Only ninety years, I have yet a lot of time." But when it comes to pleasure and sensory satisfactions, "After all, Chari, how much can a man live, ninety years? Well I have enough time, you know, what is the problem? Let me enjoy this life first. I have a wife and children, and you know how it is." I am supposed to know it, you see. And having to be courteous in Western society in Occidental places, naturally I put on a weak smile and say, "*Jawohl*," or "Of course," or "*Bestimmt*," or whatever it is, "*Bien sur*," and grieve in my heart, smile in my face and walk away.

That is a moment of danger. Babuji used to say that at that point, if you look after the abhyasi, speak to him, be nice to him, console him, show to him the inner beauties, the inner realities, the inner verities, the ecstasy that is possible, unimaginable in scope, which lies within, nobody would look outside again. So that is the first hurdle, you see, as it were, in our *yatra*. The turning inwards of the tendencies itself is the first hurdle. If, by His grace and our wisdom and the strength of our aspiration, we cross that hurdle, you can almost say half the battle is won.

Now at least your continuance on the path is assured. You are not going to run away. You may be unsatisfied; you may call your guru names, but you will remain. You will remain because you know that inside you is something which is totally different, which is a must, whatever the external world may say. You know, it is like a child which has to eat its sandwiches because mommy says so, but it has an ice cream in the other hand, it takes a lick at this and a swipe at that and satisfies itself that it is having fun.

So we participate a little here, a little there. Slowly, this goes. Because as we meditate, and as we receive more and more transmission, the inner Reality grips us; no longer like that of a dog, which is holding onto you like a bulldog, you see, but to which now you begin to cling. You see, what was holding us has let go, and we are now holding onto it. Because we know that if we give up, now we are lost. That is when much of our ability to counsel abhyasis, to reassure them, is very essential.

Of course, many of you will say, "But Babuji never did it." He did it! Who can say he did not do it? He did it in a way which was most unobtrusive. He would gently look you in the eye and say, "Did you have your tea?" That was enough. Or, "I am telling you, you look tired. Please go and sleep." That was enough. Because we have lacked the love and the consideration of even those few words. And when we find a master who need not even look at us, but who is condescending enough, or loving enough or gracious enough to look at me and say, "You look hungry, would you like to eat something?" we begin to weep.

Actually, everybody has wept before the Master. If anybody says no, he or she is a liar. I have known no exceptions,

Stages of Spiritual Progress

including, perhaps I should say, "I am happy to say," or "I am ashamed to say," you should decide, myself. And I am supposed to be a lion! [laughter] Yes, it is nothing to be snickered at, because I have not wept, even when my mother died. Why does it affect us? You know, if you go to a Western household and they give you a plateful of spaghetti and salad, with the best olive oil on it and vinegar, from I do not know where, and grapes from Tartari, things like that, *Shakespearian bliss* — you do not feel that. Why? Because it is in a gross form. The love is no doubt there, you see, but it is gross, it is given in a material shape. He gave it to you in the subtlest form — heart to heart.

So I have often felt that to feed a man who is very hungry and famished, really, food is not necessary. Food he can find anywhere. What he wants is that gentle, loving touch. "Are you hungry, my friend? Come." And he weeps. He feels full and when you put food before him, his throat chokes up with emotion, and he cannot even swallow. That is the miracle of the sympathy of a loving heart. You do not have to weep and hug and kiss on both cheeks. How many of us are capable of that sort of, you know, almost unnoticeable, imperceptible sympathy which emanates from love personified to one who is love-craving personified? How many of us have felt it? Have you ever felt it in your human interpersonal intercourse, perhaps sometimes? That is what we yearn for, that is what we crave for, that is what we hunt the world for; either through wealth or through power or through position, or the males through the females, the females through the males, you know, this whole enchanting amusing dance of the human, it is for that, you see.

That is why when we went to Babuji we never looked back. Most of us are still here because of Him. We still treasure, we still cherish those few moments, and the memory of that holds us. Now you see, if the memory of a thing can hold you, what must have been the power of the reality itself? But how many dinners do you remember which you have had, parties you have attended? Yes of course, "I wore my taffeta of blue," that is all we remember, you see, what we wore, not what they gave. Because they gave not with the heart. They gave out of their treasuries, yes, but not from this treasury [pointing to the heart], which is what is significant.

So the preceptor must remember whatever he does or she does, put some of the heart into it. Without it the whole spiritual exercise is liable to fail — often fails. And it is almost unavoidable, because we transmit from the heart. The heart is totally involved, you see, in this spiritual game of Sahaj Marg. Whether you give or you receive, it is with the heart. Thank heavens! Because there are many who can give with the heart but cannot receive. They have fun with giving, you see. "Oh, I am a charitable person, Chari. I am a philanthropist. I like to give." "Oh, would you like to have a slip of..." "Oh, I have enough of them, you know, gilt-edged, printed, embossed." That is why I have often said, "To receive is even more difficult than to give." Because receiving needs a lack of the ego. Giving gives us pride, gives us satisfaction. When we have to give we like to give, because we want to be givers. "Oh, I donated this, Chari. You know this whole six hundred hectares. When my old man died I said, 'Well, let me give something away. Let his soul rest in peace.'" The Americans are expert at this sort of thing, creating foundations for the poor — millions of dollars. But there is no heart there, you see. A million dollars without this [pointing to his heart] is dust and ashes. And give nothing at all, but give **this** [pointing to his heart], it is everything in this world. So when we transmit with the heart, from the heart, why not also give something by way of this mouth, with the heart? Speak lovingly, listen lovingly.

Stages of Spiritual Progress

And here comes the great, you know, problem that to speak is easy, to listen is very difficult. One has to be trained to be a listener. To listen is not an easy thing. Because in listening we are passive, our egos have no chance of flaunting themselves. We cannot show off. We cannot pretend. We are what we are, you see, very much like a corpse. But when somebody comes to you, you have to listen. Very often you do not have to do anything more. Just listen twenty minutes, thirty minutes, two hours. And in their telling of their tale and the shedding of a few tears, their misery is worked out of their system, you see, and they go back clean, praising your name, praising your Master. For what? For listening, you see.

So please learn to be patient. Learn to listen. It is too easy to give advice without listening but it is a waste of time for both of us. Listen patiently. Very often we do not have to do anything more. And that saves us the embarrassment of telling them something which may be right or not. Asking them to do something which may be advisable or not. If you can relieve them of ninety-eight percent of their misery by just listening, the other two percent is inconsequential. They can bear it. They can support it. In fact, it is like the salt in food, **necessary**. Because as Babuji said, "Some misery is necessary to keep us oriented towards divinity." When we are miserable we think of Him. When we are happy we never think of Him, we forget Him. So that two percent which remains is a blessing in disguise for that person.

So you see, this is the stage, when we have to turn inwards, that the danger comes, the first hurdle comes. I think it is the biggest hurdle, too. Because, subsequently there are only hurdles of the path. This is a hurdle imposed by ourselves upon ourselves. Then comes, you know, the grand possibility of moving from the first point to the second, to the third, to the fourth. The fifth we bypass, because it is a region attributed to illusion, *maya* as we say in Sanskrit. And if a person is allowed to stay there he develops hallucinations, illusory tendencies, things like that, and he will destroy himself. So it is only a transit, you see. Sometimes it is only going, skirting around that point.

Perhaps I should draw another sketch. What happens is, here you have the fifth point, and the third, and the fourth — moves from here [point one to point two], here [point two to point three], here [point three to point four], and then we just go and like this go to this point [point four to point seven], the cosmic. Without touching the forehead also, which is not of importance in the Sahaj Marg system. That is why sometimes you will find abhyasis of a certain advanced state, they report that they felt pressure in the temples or a tickling in the temples. It is a very significant experience — that now the motion of the inner self is going from here, like this, through the temples,

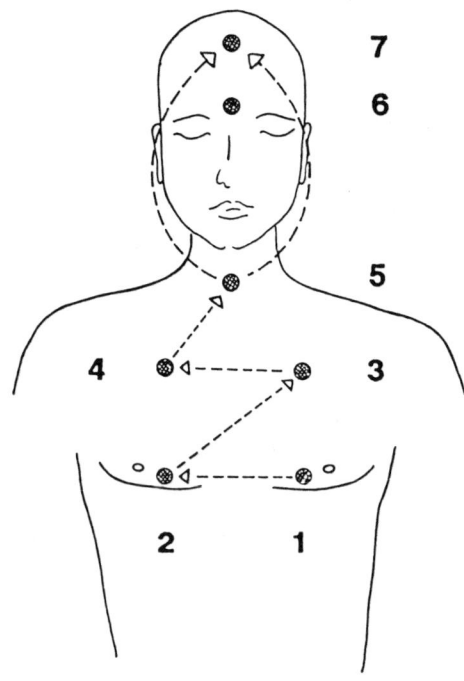

Stages of Spiritual Progress

here. And when you reach this point that is the state, the first hold on the mental region; the heart region has been traversed.

Now the heart region Babuji described as the gutter of humanity. Gutter, sewers, you know, all the filth, all the grossness, all the muck, it is deposited here. And the cleaning is absolutely the most difficult in the heart region. Rome was not built in a day, as they say! We have to have patience and faith in ourselves, and in the Master's power. It is difficult.

You know, if you ask a man to open that manhole and go in and wash out the sewer which is choked inside, very few people would like to do it. It stinks, does not it? The first time I had such an experience it was totally without any volition on my part. It was something automatic. There seemed to open up an enormous sewer here, you know, sewer pipe, something like eight feet in diameter: two metres, two and a half metres. And out of it was gushing the most sordid mess that you can imagine: nasty things, vile things, vicious things, effluence. And giving a sitting to that abhyasi I was so nauseated that I was almost compelled to vomit there and then. But I was able to control myself. And then when I reported it to Master, it happened in Shahjahanpur, in his house, he said, "That is the condition of that abhyasi, you see. I am glad you were able to open it up." He did not sympathize with me, you see. [laughter] He said, "I am glad you were able to open it up. Now look at the abhyasi's face." And I tell you, his face was transformed, you know, totally transfigured, an ecstatic appearance on the face. He felt a lightness he had never felt before. It is like when you have a boil which is ready to burst, you know, pling, pling, pling, with every beat of the vein or the artery, it is crucifying you almost. And a single lance by the surgeon, you know, with his scalpel, and instant bliss! You are asleep, because all that pus, you know, is out. This is the pus of existence, of manifold existences we carry here. We are worried about the external boils of the skin. What about the inner boil, which is full of the pus of millions of existences of the past? How nasty must it be, how corrupt, what a stink it must have.

It is not surprising that very often we are ashamed of ourselves. We are unable to look ourselves in the face in a mirror, and suicidal tendencies develop. Not because of psychological theories, you know, which say: this and this and this draw him to suicide. It is always the case of inner revulsion against the self. That is the yogic truth. When I cannot face myself, when I can no more live with myself, I destroy myself in the futile hope that the self, which is destroying the other Self within it, can exist by itself. It finds out, too late, that it has participated in the ultimate desecration possible in this universe, annihilation of the Self. Therefore suicide is the ultimate crime for a spiritual person; it is the ultimate crime. There is no redemption, because you are working against the laws of the Creator, the laws of Nature, which say, "Life shall be preserved." And in this context I would like to remind you of Lalaji's saying that, "Human life must be preserved at all cost." Because, whatever may be its current stature, its state, nevertheless it is at the summit of evolution as we know it today.

And it is destined to evolve further. So if you sort of grapple it in the throat and finish it off, you are interfering with the evolutionary forces of Nature. Not only are you killing yourself, but you are interfering with the overall scheme of evolution. Who knows, you may be the next saint! The child you abort stupidly could have been another personality. Therefore yogic science says, "You can conceive, but you cannot destroy." You have the right not to conceive, you see, but once conceived you are no more master of that child growing in your womb than anybody else. It is not yours any more! It has come into an existence where it is now God's. You are only a trustee looking after it during its existence, during **your** existence,

Stages of Spiritual Progress

doing the best possible to make of it what its maker wanted to make it. 'Maker' implying not you but Him. Therefore, abortion is, spiritually speaking, a crime. Murder, if you will have it. I mean, whatever the medical profession may say, the church may have to say, it is irrelevant. It is a spiritual truth, we have to accept it.

Now when should we start spirituality? This brings us, I mean, sequentially to the next subject. Lalaji is said to have told Babuji, "The right moment is the moment of conception when the being has come into mortal existence." **That** is the moment. But unfortunately if you are missing that moment, for various reasons, we cannot know when the child is conceived. If that opportunity is lost, then in Sahaj Marg we have to wait till the eighteenth year, because in between the child is too innocent. It does not know what it wants, why it wants, it is only forced into spirituality. But here one must come willingly. You cannot compel someone to love God, you see, or even a lover. "No, no, you love me!" Can you say to somebody? Love has to come from the heart. Therefore this tragedy of love, in even human situations, you see, that **you** love but the person you love does not love you. What can you do about it? "Oh! I love you darling! "Yes, so what! Go ahead! I am not stopping you. But do not expect anything from me." This is the law of love. So the child must know, must be mature enough to know what it wants, why it wants it, and to be able to do something about wanting and getting. So eighteen is prescribed. So at the moment of conception, or at eighteen. Nothing in between, generally.

So this heart region, coming back to that mess, you see, which is the most difficult place to clean, Babuji once told me that sometimes he felt as if he was under the sewer systems of a big metropolis — nowhere to go, dark everywhere, stinking. You are afraid to fall because if you fall into that mire you will never rise again. Awful demons, imagination and reality around you. Rats! Sewer rats are supposed to be the biggest. And Babuji's face took on such an expression, you would have pitied him if you had seen it. And there was an occasion when he prayed to Lalaji, "Why have you put me in this gutter?" And Lalaji said, "Which gutter? That is in a human being and you are there to clean it. Clean it!"

And the generosity of the Master, you know, Babuji told me once that he was in a city called Benares in the centre of India, a holy city, the holiest of holy cities in India. But it has its own red-light district. Inadvertently Babuji wandered into it. He did not know where he was going. And as he was walking through those streets, Lalaji's voice came from above, "My friend, what are you doing here?" Babuji was shaken. I mean, Babuji was really shaken. He said, "*Saheb*," (*Saheb*, means Master), "I do not know where I am, I do not know what I am doing." Lalaji said, "Well, this is not the place where you should be, but since you have come, clean it."

You see, there was no choice! A broom, wherever it is, has to do the cleaning. If it is in the bedroom it cleans the bedroom. If it is in the toilet it cleans the toilet. If it is in the throne room it cleans the throne room, too. It has no choice, you see, it can only clean. Therefore Babuji said, "I am the vacuum cleaner. I clean anything that has to be cleaned." In cleaning we cannot distinguish between good dirt and bad dirt, superior dirt and inferior dirt. You know, it is like a barber shop in South Africa where they will remove the white man's hair from the floor but not the black man's perhaps. Hair is hair, you see.

So filth is filth, wherever it may come from. And our job is to clean that. Spare the Master that **effort**. Not the work, but that **effort**. In his old age it was physically beyond him to do so much for 10,000 people, 15,000 people, ever-increasing

Stages of Spiritual Progress

numbers of people. Therefore, he had preceptors who are expected to do, as I said yesterday, only the cleaning. Forget the rest. If you are able to do the cleaning properly as your Master wants it, you have rendered your Master a signal service which cannot be rewarded normally. Such service we render to him.

So please do not under-rate this cleaning. It is of the utmost significance, it is of utmost importance, even to the Master himself. Because until **you** clean, **He** cannot do anything about it. And once he had to write a letter to a centre in India from where, I think, eight or ten abhyasis had gone to be with Babuji for three days. Babuji wrote back to the head of that centre, "I am happy that you sent these people to me. I like to see my abhyasis when they come. And I like to serve them in my own way. But I am sorry that you sent them in such a sordid condition that all the three days they were here I could spend only in cleaning. I could not advance them further. I regret to say that you have failed in your duty towards me and the Mission. Had you but done the cleaning necessary, they would have benefited much by coming to me. Now that benefit has been denied." It was a very stern letter from the Master, you see, very rare! Babuji rarely wrote such letters. So you can imagine what anguish he must have suffered that those abhyasis were there, and he was not able to do anything, but could do only the cleaning!

Of course it was a great service. But normally Babuji's, what shall I say, his promise was that anybody who went to Shahjahanpur to see him was raised at least one point. That was his gift. I asked him once, "Deserving or undeserving, you do not care? He said, "No! When somebody loves me enough to take the trouble of coming all the way to see me, that one point is the minimum I can give them." Though he could not have given us saris and dresses and perfumes like we get elsewhere, he gave us immeasurable spiritual benefits, because from the first point to the second point, remember forty-five years of spiritual practice! And if he moved you just one point here, he was saving you forty-five years of the most intense, most ascetic of spiritual practices. This was his gift, you see. And when we do not clean the abhyasi who goes to him, and he has to clean him, and he cannot give them this one point rise, imagine what you have denied them, as a preceptor. Because it is our failing which denies them.

So, I cannot sufficiently emphasize the importance of cleaning for ourselves, for the abhyasis who come to us. It is of the utmost importance, there is nothing more important than that in Sahaj Marg. Transmission comes only after cleaning. You know the dictum that, "If you transmit to a thief, you will only make him a better thief. If you continue to transmit you will make him a perfect thief." Transmission without cleaning can actually damage a person. So transmission is always done only after sufficient cleaning has been done. That is why we give these introductory three sittings which are devoted solely to cleaning. No transmission at all. Sometimes it has to be more. As Babuji said, "In one case, I had to give twenty-two sittings." Now how to judge whether a man needs the three mandatory cleanings, or twenty-two, or perhaps even fifty? Who knows?

We do the work. You see, it is like a doctor. He looks at a patient, he comes to his diagnosis. It is not a judgement. It is a diagnosis. What has to be done? It is based on his reading of what he has seen in the patient. Without that how can he do his treatment? "Take an x-ray." "No, no, no, I do not want you to see my insides. I am a virgin, you know, I never uncover myself. The x-ray will show everything inside." "Okay!" But this is something the x-ray will not reveal. You can reassure the patient, "My dear girl, x-rays will not reveal what you are afraid of revealing. They will only reveal your bones. And you

Stages of Spiritual Progress

have bone cancer. I want to know where exactly it is, so that I can treat you." It is said that we should not be afraid of stripping ourselves naked before doctors and lawyers; one physically, one emotionally. We have to tell them everything that we have done if a lawyer is to defend you in court. If you hide everything that you have done and say, "No, no, you fight the case on the premise that I have not done anything," what can he do? I would add a third one. You have to be absolutely naked before your Master. There can be nothing hidden from him. And in any case, you cannot hide anything from him. He is the all-knower. What can you possibly hide? Then why is it we have to be naked? It shows that I have no more any ego, I have no more any shame, I am what I am, take me as I am! And in his benevolence, in his mercy, in his immense love for us, he says, "Come!" So you see, there is nothing to be ashamed of.

The heart region **is** spirituality, you see. Beyond it, it is also like, you know, to draw a parallel again from science, it is like when you leave the earth's gravitational fields, you are free. You do not need any motive power any more. You do not need any engines. You do not need any rockets. If you choose to stay on course, you can go on infinitely. Nothing can stop you. That is why the heart region is of such utmost importance, because in it are embodied the principles of the earth, the water, the fire and the air. Strangely enough the fifth principle of the Western mystics, the European mystics, the ether principle is missing. But in its place we have the *atman*, the soul. And here is embodied the known universe. And one who conquers this and goes beyond is free. That is why this is the point of liberation. I have gone beyond the *pancha bhutas*, as we call it, you see, the five principles of physicality, of manifestation of this universe. Beyond that I am always free, totally free.

Does evolution stop? No. Because there are other dimensions yet to be conquered, yet to be overcome, yet to be passed

Courmettes

through, traversed — the mind region and the central region. That I shall, notwithstanding my promise to cover it today, I shall cover tomorrow, because it may take a little more time. I think we have had enough for today.

Thank you.

5

Stages of Spiritual Evolution

Courmettes, France
Wednesday, July 13, 1988

Only in India, it is never 'sisters and brothers', it is only 'brothers and sisters'. [laughter] Yes, you see, in the East, I do not have to explain. [he chuckles] You all know what I mean. Though the women always come first, the men put themselves first in the East. Here also the women come first, but the men are a little wiser and they allow the women to go first. [laughter] You see, [he laughs] that is the only difference. So today we have to begin with today. [he laughs] [laughter]

Today's talk is on stages of spiritual evolution. I want that book, who has taken that book *Efficacy of Raja Yoga*? I have been reminded that we have to cover the mind region and the [he laughs] [laughter] whatever it is, you see, the central region, but it is not really important. It is rather early to discuss because most of us, we are concerned with the heart [he laughs], though we should be concerned with the heart region. So that is just a bit of humour.

The mind region, as Babuji has said, you know, it starts here actually, the point six, but we do not touch it. This is the point where, as my Master has discovered, the entire power distribution system is located. Everything that pertains to power and energy in the system, the distribution point is this [points to point six]. Therefore, we find in some systems, especially in the *shakti* path, as we call it (path means the way, you know, the *chemin*; the *shakti* is power), the meditation has been adopted at this point and you will find *tantrics* and all the other systems of hatha yoga, they all base their main emphasis, they lay their emphasis on this point. Now this has been a very misleading thing, hitherto, till Lalaji came, Babuji came, on the scene. It has been very misleading because throughout India people have been meditating on this point as the sort of, you know, the ultimate point, point of ultimate importance. And unfortunately in the Gita, the Bhagavad Gita, which is the famous text, it is not exactly a religious text as people say in the West, it is a text pertaining to human life, human evolution, where a small drama is enacted. It is set on the battlefield of the Kurukshetra, where two factions, royal factions, two branches of the same family: brothers, cousins, you see, on one side we have the five Pandavas, as they are called; on the other side the hundred Kauravas. And the kingdom belongs to the Pandavas, by right, but the Kauravas have seized it; they refuse to return the kingdom. Lord Krishna, the divine *avatara purusha* is the mediator. He tries to mediate with the Kauravas. He asks the Pandavas to give up their claim. They will not. He tells the Kauravas, "Why do not you give back the kingdom?" "No!" "At least five cities?" "No!" "Five towns?" "No!" "Five villages?" "No!" "Five houses?" Duryodhana, the eldest of the Kauravas says, "I will not give them even as much land as can be put on five pins!"

So, the war begins. And before the war begins, when the two armies are posed opposite each other, Krishna drives the chariot of Arjuna. Arjuna sees the opposite side. He sees all his blood relations, his cousins, his uncles, his, you know, the whole thing. And he becomes feeble. He loses his courage. He starts weeping. He throws down his bow and arrow and says, "I will not fight." That is the beginning, you see.

Then Lord Krishna recites, it is said, the Gita which contains seven hundred couplets. Now, Babuji said it is stupid, nobody could have the time to recite seven hundred couplets,

Stages of Spiritual Evolution

which takes about five hours, you know, in Sanskrit, while the two armies are waiting to kill each other. [laughter] And the Gita is not really seven hundred couplets long. Most of it is a later addition. According to Babuji, it is only six or seven couplets, I do not remember exactly: seven I think, or six, maybe. These are the only six, and they were not spoken, but the essence of their meaning was transmitted to Arjuna by Krishna. Krishna was the charioteer, Arjuna was the man sitting behind, the warrior.

So this is the scene in which the *Gita* takes place. Unfortunately, there Krishna refers to this point [points to point six] between the eyebrows as the point for meditation. So, it has what amounts to divine authority, divine sanction. You see, Lord Krishna, the *avatar purusha*, even today he is the reigning deity of the *Kaliyuga* which has commenced only five thousand years ago, and which has something like 4,320,000 years yet to go. Or maybe 432,000, I am not sure. But it is big enough for us not to worry about the figure. And he is the reigning deity, he is the presiding deity, he is the ruler of this entire universe during this period.

So, not only has yoga *shastra*, as defined by Patanjali, given this point for meditation, as one of the points, but the main point it emphasizes again and again; the other is the one at the end, or the tip, of the nose. The funny thing is, because of the Gita, it has derived the weight of divine authority and sanction. In the yogic literature I do not think there is any reference to the heart as a point of meditation. Because one thing is that yoga *shastra*, or what you call the body of knowledge pertaining to yoga, is mainly ascetic and stoic in its emphasis of human behaviour, human nature, the development of human tendencies. There is not much, I should even say, there is no reference at all to things like love, compassion. They are supposed to be weaknesses. And the tradition speaks of the four stages of human life. The young fellow who is a student from birth and up to the culmination of his education, who is called a *brahmachari*, he is not supposed to be married. He is not supposed to have any relationship with the other sex. He is celibate. It is called *brahmacharya*. Then he becomes a *grihastha*, which is the stage of the householder. Then the third, after he has his children and sets them up in life, he becomes what they call a *vanaprastha*, one who leaves the family, renounces everything, having fulfilled his duties, not before. The *shastra* speaks of the necessity to fulfil your duties to your wife and children, establish them, leave enough resources for them, see that they are happy, and then say, "Good-bye. Now the time comes for me to leave you. I have done what I could, what I had to. Now please let me go on my spiritual pursuit." So he goes into the jungle, lives with his wife in a hut, eats from the forest what he can: berries, roots, leaves, things like that, and practices meditation.

So you see, the yoga *shastra* begins after the family life, involvement in raising the family, human love, all this is finished with. So in a sense, the ancient yogic *dharma* of India is not really negating the need for love and compassion, but begins at a stage which transcends the stage of youth and education, acquisition of knowledge, the stage of the family, the householder, the master of the house, who has had his fulfilment in matters of love, affection, family, profession, earning enough money, everything, you see. And then around the age of forty-four, forty-five, when he has fulfilled all these things, he is supposed to have completed that chapter of his existence. Now he renounces everything and goes into the jungle. One may ask, why does the wife go with him. Not as a wife any more. Because in India we have this concept that the wife is the *sahadharmini*, one who helps you in the performance of your duties, *dharma*, that which upholds even the

Stages of Spiritual Evolution

universe. So she is the *sahadharmini*. In the ancient Vedas, they speak of the need for the wife without whom you cannot do anything that pertains to religion, rituals, prayer. The wife has always to be by your side. Another Sanskrit term for the wife is the *ardhangini*, one who is your other half. So in the Hindu concept, the husband and wife are one. They are not two separate things, two separate sexes. It is a one, becoming a two, blending into one finally, giving up all these passionate tendencies of the body and the mind. Now united together in the pursuit of a common purpose, both seeking their salvation in a jungle life, free of the trammels of civilization, free of the trammels of daily life, away from the family, no more bothered with anything except their cherished search for the Ultimate.

So you see, although apparently there is no room for love and compassion in the Hindu scheme of things, in the yogic scheme of things it is really a transcendence. Yes, you have finished with all this nonsense of love and compassion and humility and charity. Now, go ahead.

It is important to remember this because I myself was mislead when I first studied Christianity. Thanks to my education in an English school under the Protestant church, I had to attend church on many Sundays. I have attended church for some seven years. I am an expert on Christianity. I had to study the gospel of St. Mark. I had to pass an examination conducted by the Diocese of Nagpur. If I did not pass that examination, I could not appear for my final examination at the end. It was a compulsion, you see, under the British rule. It is good it was there, you see, because without it I would not be able to speak to all of you so frankly sometimes about Christianity and other things. I have even been a choir boy in church. I have sung psalms. So it was an education which I liked.

And why I say this is, because I was fascinated by this attitude of compassion in Christ. Wherever he went he was compassionate. To everything he was compassionate. I mean, if there is a keynote, if you want to know what is the keynote of Christianity, it is compassion. To my mind, I am not an expert, though I claim to be one, but to me, it is Christ's compassion which is noteworthy, which is praiseworthy, which is everything. Other than that, he had nothing. He was a carpenter and very ill-educated, poorly educated, did a few miracles here and there, and as my Master once said, half jokingly, very seriously, he had but twelve disciples, one of whom crucified him finally. This is Master's statement. So Babuji asked, "What did Christ really achieve?" And his miracles got him nowhere. His spiritual teachings, if we are prepared to believe them, he got from India in the missing years of his life, for which there is no record in the Christian lands or in the Christian tradition. But I believe there are some hidden and secret sources of information buried under the papal vaults of the Vatican which they are unwilling to release because they do not want this truth to be told, you see, that Christ himself got his teaching from a different land, from the East, from India. Because then, perhaps, there would be a run from Christianity to Hinduism. But I believe that in not telling the truth they have damaged Christianity more than they know, because there is still today a run from the church, because it has not served any human purpose.

So this question of compassion, you see, why I say this is precisely because we have to transcend this business of compassion. I have referred this to you all earlier, that it is not our business to be compassionate. We have to love. Now you must carefully distinguish love and compassion. Love is something which emanates from us. It is not something we do. "I love," is stupid, you see. What is the meaning of "I love"? Or more

Stages of Spiritual Evolution

stupid, "Love me." Is it something to be done? This is the secret of my Master's existence, that I could see in him how a human being becomes love. Whether he is a saint or a divine personality or a special personality, was to me something unnecessary, irrelevant. What is a special personality? If I could know it, I would be at least a special personality myself. I could not be less than something and know about it. I have to go beyond it to know about it. This is a fact of knowledge. That is why we say, "He has mastered knowledge," in the sense that he is beyond the knowledge itself. I cannot possibly judge something which is superior to me, you see, especially when it is another human being. That is why we need superior persons to judge our progress, our selves, our character, everything. And when I found in him, my Master, that he did not love, that is why whenever people come and tell me, "Oh, Babuji loved us so much," I am inclined to take a little stick in my hand and tap them lovingly on the shoulder and tell them, "Nonsense." In the sense that you mean it, he never loved anybody. He did not know individuals, you see. When you came before him, he saw you, not your face, not your feet, but he saw your heart.

If you have ever been before Babuji and you went into his presence, he looked like this, at your heart, looked up, got his reading, and started smoking his hookah. That was the time he needed to mull over what he had read in you and to decide what to do. I do not think he saw faces. Therefore, he did not remember names. It was not necessary for him. He knew us by our hearts. We know people by their faces. The bank knows you by your bank account. Isn't it? The barber knows you by the colour and length of your hair; the shoemaker by the size of your feet; the Master by your heart. And why? Because he was concerned with the heart. He had nothing to do with anything else. He gave from his heart. He gave to your heart. He made your heart bigger and bigger, enlarged it, or shall we say, using the Sahaj Marg language, the heart expanded, as if it is a balloon into which he blew. And then occurs this miraculous, it is not a transformation, it is not a growth, it is a change in the state of being, progressively, that I, who am a stupid individual with a tiny heart the size of a fist in an immense body weighing eighty-two kilograms, am boasting of that heart. "My heart!" You know, we are all prone to do it. "You are my heart." "My heart is yours." How many times have we not indulged in these empty, farcical expressions? That tiny heart was what the Master wanted. He has said so many times. "What do you want, Master?" "Well, I am telling you, I need nothing. But if you want to give me something, it is this tiny heart that I want." Because it was something with which he could do something.

We find that educated people, you do not really do much with them. Educated people can be good, they can be bad. They can be philanthropists, they can be criminals. They can raise crops. They can commit murders. They can be chaste. They can be adulterous. They can take drugs. They can be doctors. They can be both, sometimes at the same time, drug-taking doctors. Education has never been sufficient to change the character of the human being. In the man of character, education is a good tool, a good instrument. Like everything else. In the hands of a man of character, power is good. In the hands of a man of character, wealth is good. Everything is good in the hands of a man of character. But give any of these things, or even all of them, to one who is impure, unclean, with criminal tendencies in him, and there you have the master criminals of this world, starting with, I do not know, Ghengis Khan, after him Napoleon, Hitler, Mussolini. All very intelligent people, but their tendencies were in the wrong direction. They had hearts, too, but full of corruption, greed, lust.

Stages of Spiritual Evolution

So when you look for a master, look for a master who has no greed, no corruption, no lust, no temptation, nothing in him. Forget his education. Education you can find in the halls of the great universities — PhDs and beyond, you see, people who teach PhDs. Wealth you can find, as they say, the epitome of wealth under the cobblestones of the streets of Zurich, 'the gnomes of Zurich' they are called. It is said that under Zurich is not sewers but bank vaults. If someday somebody should atom bomb that town, perhaps you will find a million tons of gold, you would not be surprised; the wealth, especially the ill-gotten wealth, of this whole world is buried there.

So you see, like we bury the dead in tombs, we bury our ill-gotten gains in certain tombs. For the nonce it is Switzerland. So wealth, health, education, power, yoga has always tended to look askance at them, set them aside if possible. And in its writing, in its teaching you will always find a warning, especially against knowledge and power. Two things which are easily misused. And if you say, what about money? Money is power, you see. What about sex? It is also another power. So power and education, two things which corrupt the mind and its possessions. 'I' and 'mine' — two things.

Therefore, you find in the yogic literature of our great Eastern traditions, especially India, more especially Sahaj Marg, this suspicion, you see, of all that pertains to material existence, especially of power. Therefore Babuji has said, "Transmission is forceless force, there is no power in it." Because if there was power, it could be corrupted. You know the ancient dictum, "Power corrupts. Absolute power corrupts absolutely." I have often said that I do not agree with it. Yes, in the hands of a corrupt man, power corrupts him more and more. But in the hands of a pure man, power can do nothing but good.

Courmettes

I have told many of you many times, people say, "Oh, he was tempted by his friend in school and he started taking drugs." It is not possible to be tempted by anybody but our own self. Nothing in the universe can tempt someone in whom there is no samskara, there is no reflection, there is no resonance set up by what you see outside yourself. It is not possible. So where is the temptation? It is in us, you see. We react to something, and that reaction we call a temptation, and blame the thing which has caused the reaction. Well, if I did not have something here which reacted to it, God Himself could not tempt us.

Why do you have this famous myth of the temptation, whether it be of Christ or the Buddha or anybody else? At the culminating point of their meditation, either in the desert or on the mountaintop or under the bo tree, along comes Mara in the case of the one, the devil in the case of the other and Shaitan in the the case of the third, and tempts. What is the temptation? Unlimited power, unlimited life. "I give thee dominion over the lands of this world." At that moment, temptation is the most potent thing. I mean, ordinary mortals, their temptations are futile temptations, petty temptations. Because the power that resonates in you is a feeble power at most. But imagine the power of the saint who has vacuumised his heart. If he falls to temptation, he goes straight into the nethermost parts of what you call hell. I mean, there is nothing in between. Perhaps that is how Lucifer fell. And that is why he had to fall so low as to become a devil.

We cannot possibly become devils. Because we do not have the power to be a devil. Devils need powers. Devils need enormous powers. Devils need the power almost of Divinity itself in a negative direction. It is like a see-saw which balances. If there is forty kilos here, there must be at least thirty-nine kilos here to give some sort of a balance. Nothing can transcend God, because God is even, to my mind, the creator of the devil

Stages of Spiritual Evolution

himself. Because it was by His law that the devil came into being by falling from his august status of being an angel. If God wished, He could have stopped it. So, to say that there is an angel other than God, and that God Himself is fighting the powers of the angel, to my mind, please excuse me, this is one of the stupidities of Christianity. A devil can never fight divinity. It can tempt us, again as I say, the devilish tendency in us is tempted by the devil outside, and we blame the devil. "Oh, the devil came." "He sold his soul to the devil."

I was once very happy to see a video film, an American film about God and the devil. I do not remember the title, but it was a beautiful story, you see. There is a taxi going on one of these beautiful American highways and on his radio phone comes a message. And he rushes to that spot. There is a baby being born. It is just born. He rushes there. And there is an old fellow leaning against a lamppost, very scroungy looking sort of fellow, a hobo as you say in America. And he is God. Because the old mother who is giving birth to the child is dying, and she is praying to the Almighty, "God, look after my child. When I am gone, who will look after him?" In answer to this prayer, God comes as a hobo, he is leaning there, and in the taxi is the devil because his representatives have informed him that another soul is being born. "Come, hurry up. This is your opportunity." And as this boy grows, he goes into negative tendencies. And one day, he is a musician, he wants to be the best musician. And the devil comes. He says, "You want to be the best musician?" He says, "Yes." "Well," he says, "you just sign this bit of paper here, you know, and you will find you are him." He says, "Well, what have I got to do?" "Oh nothing, you see. It is a stupid thing they call the soul and nobody even knows where it is, you see. I just want you to say, 'Well, this thing I give,' you know. I am not asking you for money or wealth or anything like that. Just a stupid thing which nobody knows where it is — the soul. Who cares about the soul? Have you heard anybody talking about the soul, being worried about the soul? Their bodies, yes; their bank accounts, yes; their women, yes; soul — have you ever even heard it being mentioned?" The boy says, "No. All that I know is my music." "Yes. That is why I am here, to help you, you see. You are to be the best musician. Just put your signature here." The boy signs, and he is lost. He is transformed, you know. Next moment he finds himself as the best musician who is dethroned and thrown into the gutter. Many years later, when he is dying because he is sinning, you see, he is living another man's life; he is a vampire, created by the devil in that picture. When he is almost finished, he remembers his mother and her prayer and he says, "God, you to whom my mother prayed, please help me." And along comes God. He says, "My son, that was all that was necessary. Nothing more you need do. You thought of me, here I am. Your problems are over." And next moment he finds himself back as the person he was, with his lovely girlfriend, who is happy to welcome him back, redeemed forever by one single thought of divinity. You see, it was a most beautiful picture. I am surprised the Americans could make such a movie. [laughter] [he chuckles] Anyway, hats off to them. But if you can find it, it is worth looking at it.

Now why I give this story, you see, because Babuji has said again and again, "Think of Him and He is there." We do not have to do anything, we do not have to telephone, we do not have to press the buzzer on the computer or anything, you know, and He is there. Now this thought is obviously from the mind, therefore the importance given to the mind region in spirituality, what we call the cosmic region. [he chuckles] I am coming to it by a roundabout sort of way. [laughter] Yes. But I get there eventually. That is why the mind region is so important, but you cannot come to it until the tendencies are

Stages of Spiritual Evolution

cleared off. Even the tendency to think wrong is a tendency. Some people are always brooding over the wrong things of life, negative things of life, the dark side of life. Chronic worriers who have blood pressure problems, develop acidity, eventually heart attacks. It is not the mind's fault, it is the tendency that they have created in themselves to think of the wrong things always.

It is like that famous description. You have a glass of water half full, the pessimist who looks at it and says, "My God, it is half empty. What shall I do with this situation; a half empty glass of water? What can I ever do with it?" The optimist comes and says, "Oh, half a glass full of water, how jolly good!" The same glass of water, two different evocations. So the mind *per se* has nothing to do with what we think. I mean, there are psychologists here who might be a little astonished to hear this, but the mind *per se* has nothing to do with what we think and the way we think. The mind is an instrument. It is like blaming the telephone for an obscene call which you received at midnight. What can the telephone do? It is the man at the other end who should be blamed, or the woman sometimes. So you see, my mind is an instrument. It has nothing to do of itself, either to be blamed or praised. I am the user of the mind.

Here comes the great position that psychology, or at least yogic psychology, holds. That the mind is the first instrument of the soul. It is an instrument which is intangible, which has no physical existence, which cannot be located in space or in the body or even perhaps in time. It goes, it seems to go, with the soul. As for the brain, it is a physical thing. It is built, with the body, of cells. So we must distinguish very carefully between the mind and the brain. Intelligence, knowledge, wisdom; these things have very fine shades of meaning, shades of differences of meaning. And if we go only by the Western schools of psychology, we are liable to confuse one for the other. Often I have wondered what on earth this mind is. It is that which uses everything else, the senses, through the medium, perhaps, of the brain, the nervous system. So the mind is an intangible part of that intangible existence which we call the soul, the Self. And the region that it is supposed to control or regulate is what we call the mind region.

Now you, in English, you say mind region. We distinguish two halves of it, actually. What we call the *brahmanda* and what we call the *parabrahmanda*, you see. That is the cosmic and the super-cosmic, or the mind and the super-mind, which extends from, I think, the sixth point to the tenth or the eleventh, perhaps even the twelfth. Because there is a certain overlapping, there are no rigid boundaries possible here. And this mind is also important because Babuji has said, "It is the landing ground of the gods." That means it is perhaps that neutral territory where you and the divine can meet. You know, like when you want to sign an armistice, you specify a certain place where both the commanders can meet. It is neutral territory, white flags on either side, no firing, no shooting, nothing. No carnage. This is the point where humanity and divinity meets. This is my interpretation of what Babuji said, "This is the landing ground of the gods." And all your foreplanning, forethought, everything, occurs here first before it descends down into the physical realm of physical existence, physical achievement, physical execution. Therefore the importance of the mind region.

And because we cannot go to the mind region without cleaning the heart, because there lies the samskaras which make our tendencies, therefore the, even perhaps, superior importance of the heart region. Until I transform this, remove the samskaras to the necessary extent, not totally, but necessary extent, purify it, purify my tendencies, there is absolutely no use in acting upon the mind region. It cannot respond. There-

Stages of Spiritual Evolution

fore this sequence of heart region to mind region. In the super-mind, the super-cosmic, the *parabrahmanda*, is a yet further refinement. Now we have, technically speaking, we have gone beyond the gods. Please understand, because in the Hindu tradition, gods, as Babuji has beautifully written in *Reality at Dawn*, they are only functionaries of nature, even Brahma, even Vishnu, even Shiva. I mention the Hindu pantheon because they seem to transcend all other concepts of divinity in other religions. Here the *parabrahman* as we call it, the ultimate transcendental reality, the Truth which has no form, no name, no attributes, is God, with a capital 'G'. The others are all with a lowercase 'g'. Multiplicity of them, you see, the Hindu pantheon of gods is a very extensive thing. There are gods for practically everything in nature. But the top three, the trinity, is Brahma, Vishnu, and Shiva. Brahma the creator, Vishnu the protector, Shiva the destroyer, all straight descended from the Ultimate. That is where from the powerless, power has come; from the knowledgeless, knowledge has come; from beinglessness, being has come, to take charge of creation, its sustenance, and its ultimate dissolution.

And even in the Gita it says, even Brahma has to come down to this world and start his evolutionary path to reach the Ultimate again, that from there, he cannot reach. Therefore in the Hindu tradition, this is called the *karma bhumi*, the *bhumi*, or the earth, of doing. Doing and becoming, moving and becoming, what I told you yesterday of the *atma*, you see. Therefore karma yoga teaches how, by doing, to reach the Ultimate Divinity and becoming one with it.

So something has to be done, you see. This is the essence, the secret knowledge contained in that single phrase, karma yoga. A karma yogin is one who participates in karma. Lord Krishna says in the Gita, "Even I cannot be quiet or silent or inactive for a single instant of time, because if I were so, the universe would be dissolved." It would be shattered out of existence, you see. You can easily imagine, if you think of the atom, the nucleus and the electrons, if that weak force which is holding them together was to stop for an instant in time, the electrons would fly out, off into space. And then, with that binding force removed, the nucleus would explode into its constituent parts. Very much like if the gravitational field were suddenly to collapse, the earth would be thrown off into outer space, away from the sun. The moon will fly off in another direction. The entire galactic system would be shattered into space, you do not know where. That is the ultimate chaos, you see, when the thing which is in the Centre, holding together all things, collapses, then comes dissolution.

I say this because the Western idea of destruction is destroying from outside. Well, you can never destroy something from outside. You can destroy it in the only sense that we know, breaking it up, killing it, but not destroy it. The ultimate destruction comes always from inside. This is something even Western science, perhaps military science, should take cognizance of. By guns you achieve nothing, you only allow the soul to go on its further transmutation into other regions, into other lives, into other existences, and perhaps they do a duty, too, there, a salutary obligation.

So this is the mind region, you see. And now, how does the mind work? Because using the mind, we do our reading. Doing the reading, we do the cleaning. By doing the cleaning, we make it possible for the soul of the abhyasi to start on its onward evolutionary path, commence its *yatra*. Therefore comes the need to purify the mind; first the heart — clean the tendencies. Without purifying the tendencies, the mind cannot be purified. Therefore, next the mind. And it is an interesting thing that here we see the absolutely unavoidable operation of the law of invertendo: that where in the heart we have the two halves, the upper and the lower, the upper in the upper, where we should naturally look for it, and the lower in the lower, here [pointing to the forehead], it is reversed. The upper region of the mind is actually in the lower physical side, and the lower is in the upper side. So preceptors, whenever you are able to rise to that level of action, performance, please remember to look for the higher in the lower; otherwise, you will not find it. And in passing I should also mention, when you go to the central region at this point, number thirteen, it is again reversed: the higher is again in the higher, the lower in the lower. So we have to remember, you see, that we have to sort of inverse ourselves. Very much like when you look through a pinhole, things are upside down, topsy-turvy.

Now if everything emanates here, the landing ground of the gods is here, divine action itself emanates from the cosmic, not from the Centre, you see, please remember this, the Centre is inoperative. I mentioned this in one of my talks, I think, in Vorauf, that having set this creation going, the work of the Ultimate is over. Now it is left to the masters, including the *avatars*, special personalities, to govern this universe. Some people took objection to it. They said, "How can God cease to be active? How can God cease to be involved in His creation?" If you remember the definition of God, that He is Nothingness, the Absolute of Nothingness, He has no mind, He has nothing: no power, no knowledge, no wisdom, no wealth, nothing, how can He ever possibly participate in His universe? At that time, there were many people who thought, you know, I was trying to, sort of, aggrandize the role of the Master, for personal reasons. But, please be assured, it is the teaching of my Master. And it is very simple, if you look through *Efficacy of Raja Yoga*, you will find that the landing ground of the gods is in the mind region at this point. From there, in thought form, they release the forces that take final culmination in the physical world in the form of action and results. Therefore if we wish to change our destiny, as we call it, our future, build it afresh, renew it, we have to work with our thought, with the mind. Therefore raja yoga operates with the mind, through the mind. That is why we have to meditate. That is why meditation, though it is only regulation of the mind, is very necessary, very vital. Because the mind has to be under our regulatory control. Otherwise, it runs amok. Like an elephant that has gone *must,* as we say, and it is destructive.

Therefore Babuji said, "The mind is the only thing that can redeem the human being. It is also his only source of self-destruction." Like everything on earth, it has two edges, you see, a double-edged sword. A knife to cut bread with or to cut a throat with. Money to buy a book with, or to get drunk with. Powers are always double-edged things. Therefore Babuji's greatest piece of wisdom was to avoid power totally. Absolutely, there is no power system in Sahaj Marg.

I remember once he was asked, I think in Munich, by several people, "Babuji," or "Master," someone said, "there are so many systems, there is Buddhism, there is Hinduism, there is Islam, and so many other things, you see. Which of these systems do you like best?" I was happy this question was asked, because I had been waiting for my Master to stumble, at least once, you know. Every disciple has this unholy, rather devilish desire to see his Master stumble, [laughter] at least once, you know. It makes him human. And I said, "Well, today the old man has got it. [laughter] How is he going to get out of this question? This is a beautiful trap, a beautiful question." And I was all agog, waiting for Master to make a fool of himself. But you know, he was **He.** I cannot say anything more. He put on his glasses as if he was going to look very erudite, read something, and he said, "I am telling you, I like that system in which no power is employed." It was a real answer; it was also

Stages of Spiritual Evolution

an evasive action he undertook in the face of the *blitzkrieg* of the enemy. [laughter] [he laughs] Very delightfully beautiful, wise, and only Babuji could have given such an answer. "I like that system best, in which no power is used." And actually, of course, he is saying, "My system is the best." Because in this system alone there is no power. That was his humility, his transcendental wisdom, his astonishing humour, you see, that he could convert a situation which was absolutely against him, to his benefit. Not just benefit, in which he could just finish off the enemy. And I was dumb-struck, you know.

That day my love for him, not regard or respect, because regard and respect are human things, you see (love I believe, is divine), my love for him grew a million-fold. This old person, you know, without education, in a land foreign to him, which, permit me to say, in which he was not very happy, never very comfortable, because he found so much grossness, so much sickness of the mind, soul. He was always unhappy in Europe, though outwardly he was very happy. He has told me on several occasions, "Why has Lalaji sent me into this gutter of humanity?" And then he would himself smile and say with amusement, "It is his work I am doing, you see, therefore I should not judge." And there to be confronted by the brilliant minds of the West, the educated minds, the polished minds and just, you know, in an instant to overthrow them, it was magnificent.

Now, such a mind can only, such an answer can only come from a mind purified of all trivialities of existence, opposites of knowing and not-knowing, of wisdom and un-wisdom, of intelligence and foolishness. It can come only when the Source descends to answer a question. Therefore, we say in India that all wisdom comes from linking yourself to that source. It does not come out of books. Shakespeare has said no doubt, "That out of books and running brooks, come sermons and stones." Yes, at the lower level, at the Shakespearean level, at the level of the poet, of the dramatist, of the artist, we get from here [pointing to the head]. I am not by any means decrying that, or trying to denigrate that knowledge, but it is, after all, from below us. We are superior to it.

It is like the tree which draws its sustenance from the earth, from below, but its living oxygen comes from above. From here it gets its minerals and whatnot, from above it gets the oxygen, which is the rarer, more pure, more subtle form of its nourishment. Like we draw our food from the physical sources but our breathing comes from an ethereal source, let us say, and without which we cannot live. You can live without food for months on end, two months, three months, or, on very little, perhaps for years. But can you live without breathing? How long? So you see, the subtler the level, the more dependent we are on it, the more necessary it is for us. Not just necessary, more vital for us. Therefore, air is vital, food is necessary. Happiness, yes or no, it does not matter. And when we put happiness first and necessities next and vital things last, we are inverting the whole process of existence, and suffering as a consequence. So this, please remember, we are living in a topsy-turvy way. The world is not topsy-turvy. We are topsy-turvy. We put happiness and pleasure first, sustenance and health and all next, and the vital things of existence last.

Sahaj Marg, by just, you know, sort of turning us upside down, says, "My friend, reverse yourself, put first things first. We are not saying no happiness, but start with the vital thing. What is most vital to you? Purity, truth, divinity — **start there**. Build that in you, then the other things follow. Without that, these things really do not exist. It is an ephemeral existence, an illusory existence." So without the pure mind, purified after the heart region has been purified, the tendencies having been set right, and a connection with the Master established through one's heart with His heart, all these things become impossible.

Stages of Spiritual Evolution

So you see, that is the immense importance of the mind region. And of course the other half of it, the super-cosmic mind, is only a further refinement of the same thing. But as I said, please remember, there we are now dealing with regions which transcend the regions of the gods themselves. That is why, perhaps — why perhaps? — surely, traditional worship is not recommended in Sahaj Marg, because it is unnecessary. How can you worship someone whom you have already transcended? It is not that we are more powerful than gods, or we are better knowing than gods. Not at all. We are in a different region. Like a man who is flying is in a different element from a man who is walking on the ground. This is *terra firma*, yes; but he is higher than me, in that sense. He may be poorer, he may be foolish, he may be sick. It may be a sick man who is carried on a stretcher in the plane, but nevertheless he is in a higher region. He is in a finer region, he is in a more rarefied region.

By that standard of comparison, every Sahaj Marg abhyasi who has reached the *parabrahmanda mandal* has already equalled the divine existence in its essential feature, that we are now in one region, and when we go beyond, the gods are left below us. Below, again please remember, not in a situational or quality-oriented sense, but in the absolute sense of dimensionality. Like two dimensions are inferior to three dimensions of space. So this is important.

And then we come to the central region where, as Babuji said, we are now swimming in the ocean of bliss, the seven rings of splendour. It is now in direct contact with the ultimate source, the Centre. Questions of progress cease, because it is an ever-swimming — it can never end. We are ever going towards the Centre, and as Babuji said on several occasions, "My Master is swimming before me, and passing on his achievements to me." There is still this question of achievement, you see, not in the sense of worldly achievement, but in some higher mystical, spiritual sense. Something is gained but it is being given away instantly. So why achievement? I do not know. It is perhaps part of the drama, you see, that we have to take and give. So that process of taking and giving, taking and giving, is continued, I do not know for how long.

But having completed yesterday's topic, [laughter] [he laughs] that is where yesterday I should have ended, we have to come to liberation, realisation and mergence, you see, because this is a very important topic.

Does the Centre, therefore, represent our goal? It would appear from a reading of Master's books, especially this *Efficacy*, you know, that the Centre is our goal. Very confusing, because I have known people who are in the central region having missed their way, subsequently fallen, because they thought the Centre was the goal. I told Babuji, "This is very unfair." You know, because he wrote to one person, "I have now put you in the central region and have connected you to God. Your future is now in His hands." Babuji was quite, very beautifully, lovingly, softly cruel. Because this sentence condemned that poor man. He was happy. He said, "Ah, I am now in contact with the Divinity." And his fall started. I said, "Babuji, are you not doing a disservice?" He said, "Look, I am telling the truth. I have put him in touch with God." I said, "Why has he fallen?" He said, "Because he has forgotten his Master, who put him in touch with God."

Here comes the great secret of Sahaj Marg, of our spiritual way. **You can never do without the Master.** Please remember this; please tell your abhyasis. What is the need for the Master? Well, to start the process, to clean the heart, the regions, the points, to give transmission, to improve their quality, the essence of their existence, put himself into them. It is called the

Stages of Spiritual Evolution

prana-ahuti because he is pouring his life into our life. It is an offering of his life into our life. *Ahuti* is the ancient Sanskrit word for the sacrificial offerings put into the fire of the *homa*, which is built in a very ritualistic sacred way and into which you offer the *ahuti*.

Here, our heart is the flaming heart, flaming with desire, flaming with lust, flaming with so many things, you see, into which, from his divine heart he pours his blessings. And I suppose he cools and puts out these fires and normalizes this heart, makes it human, then makes it begin its commencement of the divine *yatra* which, incidentally, is what he meant by saying, "From animal man to human man to divine man is the path." This is the secret, you see, that starting there, even after he puts you in touch with God, he is a very necessary person. We cannot afford to forget him. Yes, I connect you with, let us say, the Courmettes director and I go away. He makes you wait for two hours and says, "*Oui, Madame, Bonjour, ça va?*" and then he says, "I have some work, will you please come day after tomorrow." The man who brought you here is gone. This man is just, you know, sort of brushing you away, very politely, in French. What should I do? This is the situation of the abhyasi who thinks he has got God now, and he can do without the Master. Because God again, you see, remember, He has no mind. He cannot welcome you. He cannot recognize your presence. We need the Master till the ultimate completion of this *yatra*. That will show you where the real goal lies.

I emphasize this because many of us are happy with liberation. Liberation is, as Babuji has said, "It is the toy in the hands of a child." He said it can be given in one second; by one blink of his eyebrows Lalaji could do it; just like that, and you are liberated. That is liberation. But many people, especially in India, where yogic science deals with this concept of *mukti*, you see, which only means liberation from the travails and troubles of this worldly existence, they are after *mukti*. Yes. It is like for a sick man, he wants relief from pain, first, you see, then he wants health, then he wants happiness. But that is only an immediate need of a suffering person. For a wise person, there is no suffering, there is no enjoyment. He is after the real goal of human life. "Thou art the real goal of human life."

So you see, the prayer indicates very, very clearly, very unambiguously what is the real goal of human life, and the words 'real goal' must be taken particular note of. Why did he use the words 'real goal'? Why not just say 'goal'? Because there are so many goals, you see. Hinduism talks of *purushathas*, which are the things that are desirable, for which human beings live and die: *dharma, artha, kama, moksha*. *Dharma* is duty, *artha* is wealth, *kama* is desire and its satisfaction, *moksha* is liberation. Unfortunately they did not put the fifth, which should have been essentially there. Hinduism missed the boat. Somewhere it missed the track, you see, because by virtue of having gone into the ritualistic path, temple worship, I think it became decadent. Not now, thousands of years ago.

The Church has only begun to become decadent yesterday, if you look at it in terms of history. Hinduism has been decadent for thousands of years, therefore out of decadent Hinduism came a Buddha, came a Mahavira, who set up divergent religions. And Buddha made the mistake of going to the other extreme and negating God and saying it is only emptiness. Which was another mistake. It is like the swing of the pendulum from one extreme to the other; it served no purpose. Buddhism does not exist in the land of its birth today, and it is a decadent form of religion wherever it exists, more idolatrous than even Hinduism, which it revolted against, and which it reviled from. So you see, from a decadent religion a new thing was born

Stages of Spiritual Evolution

which in turn became decadent. That is perhaps the fate of religions, you see.

Now what happens here? God, as a religious symbol, is set aside. "Thou art the real goal." Of course, Babuji himself says, in all his humility, which we know very well, he says in, I think, *Reality At Dawn,* **He** is the real goal, we are only His representatives on earth. But it is my direct experience, you see, I have no hesitation in saying it, I have experienced the presence of my Master as the presence of the Ultimate! Now, how I experienced that, I am not interested in telling you that, because it is not relevant really. You see, I experienced this not once, but several times.

And this mistake of thinking that the Master and God are two separate things, and having got God I could negate my Master and leave him behind, was made by several persons, many of whom do not know Sahaj Marg today. Very tragic, having reached the central region, almost, some of them; one of them Babuji said would be the first man ever in Europe to touch or set his foot in the central region! He never made it, because he thought, it is like my saying, "Oh, the plane is landing at Nice." I am happy, and the next moment the plane is crashing. It is not enough if you are near your destination, however near you may be.

It is no use if I take off in Delhi and cover eight hours and twenty-nine minutes of flight to Frankfurt, and when landing at Frankfurt airport my plane crashes and I am dead. That I die on German soil does not make any difference to my spiritual journey. Am I at my destination or not? If not, it is better I am at home. Either at home or at the destination. In between, I am peaceless, I am restless, I am torn between the then and the now, between the when and the what and the where. You see the restlessness when we travel. We are happy when we are leaving but we are miserable on the way. "When will I reach? When will I reach?" You are looking at the clock and the speedometer. Why this restlessness? To be home. And to my experience, my personal experience, absolutely convincing, I have no doubt about it whatsoever, the Master's heart is my goal, you see. Not the Master, because the Master is a physical form and, as I told you yesterday, it is bound to go, but his heart is eternal. That is why Master has said, and which many have misunderstood when he says, "The heart extends from the tip to the toe." You see, he did not mean that it is the region of the heart. Why only the tip to the toe of this existence? Of the divine existence itself. The heart has to expand until the universe is within that heart. And then you can say you and I and all of us are there. In one sense. In one sense we are already in that heart, his divine heart, his immense universal heart.

Then what is the journey about? Why are we struggling with spirituality and cleaning and transmission and seminars? Utterly wasteful of our time. Demanding our patience. What for? We have to realise that we are there. Therefore, the spiritual path talks of **realisation**, not of achievement or anything else — realisation, self-realisation. The realisation that I, who am looking for someone, have that someone within me, and that someone within me is Him and myself too, this realisation dawns at the end. Therefore, liberation is an absolutely insignificant step on the path of spirituality. Perhaps desirable to those who are happy with limited goals; who only want to transcend or overcome the frustrations of a physical existence. Yes, like a prisoner in jail wants to go out, you see, first. "When will I be let free?" It is liberation. Having come out he is bewildered. If he has been a lifer, he does not know where to go. His family is dead. He has no friends. The city has changed. Even the streets have been relaid. The buses that used to operate do not have the same numbers, the tram lines are no

Stages of Spiritual Evolution

more. Where will he go? Sometimes, such prisoners prefer to get back into jail again. That is the only security, the only home they know.

So our soul, if we have not that possibility of escape or, shall we say, of liberation, then we have to come back. Because I think this is the only thing we know, you see. "Here," we think, "is the ultimate pleasure, the ultimate happiness." Many people have said, especially in Europe, "Oh, Chari, I would like to come again and again into this world. What is wrong with it?" They are prisoners who are happy in their imprisonment. Such persons, how to raise? I do not know. How to convince them that, "You are a prisoner?" It is impossible. Because he thinks he is happy. He thinks he is wealthy. He thinks he is wise. He thinks he is everything. For such persons we can only pray, "God help them."

So to our abhyasis, especially to our preceptors, I say, "Please do not go for liberation." It is like a man who is on his journey from Delhi to Frankfurt saying, "Oh I am over Karachi. Fine. I have crossed one seventh of my journey." Not at all. The journey could end right there. The beginning can never be got back again. The end is now the only thing left for us. In between there are only way stations, no use to us, you see.

So please remember, liberation — yes and no. Yes to those who want only a limited goal; relief from mortal existence. Well for them, poor souls, Master used to give it as a gift. They did not have to meditate. I have had three personal experiences after Babuji's *mahasamadhi*, where people have been blessed by being liberated in this existence. And that shows the power works, you see, that the Master never dies. It is his power which works always, you see, whether you transmit or I transmit, it is still the Master's power. Whatever it may be, powerless power, yes, but still something is working.

So what next after liberation? Let me see, [he chuckles and looks at the agenda sheet] [laughter] Realisation, you see. [laughter] [he laughs] Yes, because, you know, it is like Babuji who wrote *Reality At Dawn,* and once we were talking about this cosmic hierarchy of workers for the Master, working at different levels. And he wanted to see the book in which it was described. I gave him a copy of *Reality At Dawn,* he put on his glasses, went through the paragraph and said, "This is beautifully written. Who wrote it?" [laughter] So I showed him the cover page. Ram Chandra. He said, "Ram Chandra? You mean I wrote it?" I said, "Yes." He said, "You see, sometimes I also do good work." [laughter] So we have to remind ourselves to remember something that we have forgotten, you see. That is also an aspect of constant remembrance.

So we come next to the stage of realisation. Where we have realised that the Master in me, and the Master outside me, and I, we are all the same, you see. It is an act of realisation, not of becoming, not of growing into something. The ultimate veil of ignorance is removed from our consciousness, and there we are. But nevertheless we are still separate from him. See, as long as we have to say, "He and I are one," the 'He' and the 'I' are still existing. Therefore the final state is the one we call merger, in Sanskrit it is called *layavastha,* becoming one. The two becoming one. The grand climax of spiritual life, indeed of all life, is that merger in the Beloved.

Now I had an experience once, maybe I have written somewhere, in a transmission Babuji gave me. It was like one of these astronauts, you know, in the space vehicle, moving leg first in a weightless atmosphere. I found myself weightless, moving with my feet and entering Babuji here [pointing at the forehead]. And about one third of me entered when he said, "That's all." I was very upset, you see. I thought he had cheated me and I told him so. I said, "Babuji, *aapane hame dhoka dia*

Stages of Spiritual Evolution

(You have cheated me today)." Babuji laughed. He said, "What happened?" I said, "Well, this is what happened. I went in one third and what about the rest?" He said, "You know, this is a very good sign. Lalaji's grace. Your merger in me to the extent of one third is complete. Congratulations." I said, "For what? You have denied the other two thirds." Now that is the pessimistical attitude all over again. He said, "My friend, at your stage of development, this one third is far, far too much."

You see, here comes the important message of the Master. That development according to the points and the regions has nothing to do with the ultimate climax of spiritual existence, the merger. The merger can be today, even if you are the worst sinner in the universe, if in that instant you have this total love and the total longing to be one with him, he opens the door.

So there are many of these mystifying facets, you see. Which is true? Which is relevant? Which should I look for? If you look to the books and go by the maintenance manual, well, yes, you start with point one, then the *atma chakra*, then the fire point, then the water point, then the air, the point of illusion, then you go region by region by region. You know, it is a soul-killing journey, I should say, though it is not. I mean, to me it looks like that. What is all this for?

You see, I had once an experience in meditation. It is moonlight, twilight/moonlight, you know, the sun has set, it is twilight, and the full moon is rising, the landscape is bathed in moonlight. I am going on a road. I suddenly find myself on an elevated road and I see in the distance it is a bridge. Here it is wide as this plain and the bridge is narrowing. And it is going on and on, you know, twisting and turning, endless. So I asked Babuji what it is. He said, "That is the endless path which you are treading now." I said, "Have you given me this vision to frighten me or to encourage me?" He said, "It depends on you.

If you are frightened by it, well, it is frightening. If you are encouraged by it, it is encouraging." I said, "Babuji, do not indulge in these tricks. What exactly does it mean?" He said, "The path is long." "Yes," I said, "I have seen it in my vision, I do not need your erudition to point it out to me." Then he smiled again, he said, "You are intelligent. Think for yourself."

That night I thought long, you see. And it is strange, but the next morning, it was the very next morning that I had this experience that I woke up at four o'clock and Babuji was in the next cot, you know. I could touch him, in a small room, some of you may have seen it inside, where there used to be a wash basin and a small veranda of four and a half feet long and inside that cubicle there we were two of us side by side. I could not remember his name. I was tortured, you know. I was thinking and thinking and thinking, I could not remember his name. Waking, not dreaming. Waking. Then I thought, the beautiful thought came to me, you see, his Master's name is the same as his, let me remember his. I could not. For about forty minutes I was torturing myself.

Babuji suddenly woke up and he wanted to go to the toilet, I took him there, and then he always washed his hands and his face. And when he washed his face sometimes he used to shyly look into the mirror, you know, and his nose was bent like this. And in the mirror it was always bent in the other way. [laughter] And sometimes I think he distrusted the image because he used to look like this, you know. [laughter] To set it right perhaps. And then from the reflection he looked at me and said, "So early in the morning and you are so much worried. What is it about?" I said, "Babuji, I am not worried, I am terrified, you see, something has gone wrong. Last night you told me that I am in such and such a region and this morning, you know, I am horrified, I cannot remember your name, I cannot remember your Master's name. I have gone into some hell, you know, in

Stages of Spiritual Evolution

this night. Wet face, wet hands, beard dripping water, he hugged me. He just turned around and hugged me. I said, "What is this about, you know, you are hugging me early in the morning? What is the reason?" He said, "Today it has been revealed to you that the real Master has no name, no form, and that Lalaji and I are one. You see, that is the goal of life." So the previous evening's experience of the long, long, long, you know, unending bridge, going into the distance of space and time, frightening, was answered the next morning.

So, "Thou art the real goal of human life," is a pregnant sentence, you see, for one who can understand. But of course, you see, people say, "Oh, yes Chari, of course, you know, we need a Master. The old man is very nice, you know, he gave me a sitting this morning and by jove it was something." "What did you feel?" "Oh, you know, I felt a little vibration, I think I felt something here. I must write it down and then I will remember it." The man who cannot remember it before he has written down, how is he going to remember it after he has written it? How is he going to write it down? This is the impact the Master has on most of us. When the very first sentence of the prayer absolutely openly, unambiguously, truthfully, says what is your goal.

So that is where the spiritual journey ends. You see, it is not our fault, it is not the fault of the human being, that we cannot understand that sentence until we become that which he wants us to become. Which, incidentally, is how we know things. You cannot know anything until you have become that. You can taste an apple but you cannot know what is an apple until you become an apple. The greatest saints of this world, especially in India, you see, have not stopped their practice by just meditating and prayer and all these trivialities of spiritual existence. To me they are trivial, you see. They try to become.

Courmettes

It is said of Ramakrishna Paramahamsa, the great Master of Swami Vivekananda, that he lived as a woman for six months in the women's quarters, wearing a sari, cooking, washing utensils, sweeping the floor. And if I may be permitted to say so, tradition says he even started menstruating. His mergence in the female principle of existence was so complete, you see, that he became a female.

So, we are saying, "Oh, I practise constant remembrance several times a day, Chari." As I said, you know, the American boy told me last year, "Oh Chari, I practise constant remembrance several times a day." I said, "It is very nice, but please, try to practise it a few more times if possible." [he chuckles] [laughter] What else can you say?

Now his being the beloved, you know, is the culmination of our journey whether we enter into him or he enters into us. Yes, there is a distinct difference. Because there is this symbology in the Eastern tradition, the Hindu tradition, of the cup of water being poured into the ocean, and it becomes part of the ocean. But the ultimate achievement of spiritual practice is supposed to be where the ocean comes into the cup. So both are cases of mergence, you see. In one the soul merges in the Master, in the other the Master merges in the aspirant. And Babuji told me this long ago when we were talking of his successor. He said, "All the abhyasis today, of the past, of the future, can achieve this *laya*, where they enter into the Master. But the miracle of the Master entering into the abhyasi can only be in one case, that of his Representative," you see, who will be **him**, you see, in a real sense, because the Master is in you, you become the Master or whoever it is, at that moment.

So this ultimate principle is in two categories: one is open to all, the other one is open only to that poor fellow, whether he is cursed or blessed, I do not know, who is, shall we say,

Stages of Spiritual Evolution

fated (I do not like the word 'destined', it smacks of good things), who is fated to be his Representative, to suffer. But it is the greatest blessing to suffer. I told some Christian friends, "You are Christians but you do not know the meaning of suffering." They said, "Chari, how can you say that?" I said, "When Christ said, 'Suffer them to come unto me,' what exactly did he mean? Permit them to come to me, you see; allow them to come to me." Suffering is the permission the Master gives for us to enter into him. Through suffering we are closer to him. By the ultimate miseries of this world of suffering we become him. You see, this is celebrated in the Christian crucifixion where he gave his life for all the future Christians. Unfortunately it is limited to Christians. Perhaps fortunately, I do not know, otherwise I may not be here!

But you see, this Ultimate which transcends even realisation (realisation is a very high feature of yogic practice, yogic self-achievement, the knowledge of the self), but the Ultimate thing is this mergence in the Master. It is within our control. It is something which we can aspire for, which we can achieve. Because when I had this miraculous experience of going one third into him, and when Babuji certified, you see, that it was one third mergence in him, I had not yet left the heart region. It was way back in 1966; and there is the opposite very sad miracle also, that people in the central region have not merged with the Master.

So you see these regions have nothing to do with the actuality of the spiritual adventure, its romance, its beauty, I do not know what word to use, you see. It is a romance, you see. Spirituality is a romance; but a romance full of misery, you see, where the soul of the aspirant is torn with longing, love, separation. And when you do achieve the union with the beloved you find you are lost, you are no more there to, shall we say, enjoy that union. So sometimes we are tempted to ask,

"What is this all about?" It seems to be stupid, you know, that two people who are longing to be together, to become one, in that very act of becoming one, the yearning one has been annihilated, as it were. But you know, how can you be annihilated when you are in the Master now? That we have been outside him, thrown out of him by our stupidity, by our crass ignorance, by our self-seeking adventurous life, was the misery. To go back home into that infinite home, that infinite heart which is nothing but love, how can it ever be misery? You see, it is the aspect of dualism that still pervades our existence, that until there are two to enjoy there is no enjoyment. One cannot enjoy by himself or herself, therefore we seek ever a companion, a mate. But here there is no mating, there is union without mating, there is oneness, no more separation, no more the haunting phantasms of the night, "I am alone, I am lonely." Now all that is left behind, He and I are one. You all remember that famous Persian couplet quoted in, I think, *Reality At Dawn*, or *Truth Eternal*, where Babuji has written in Persian what Lalaji told him, "I have become you and you have become me." See, both are being used, it is not enough if I become him, he must become me.

So when the Master merges with his servant, his devotee, his lover, each has become the other. That is the beauty of the spiritual ultimacy, the ultimate goal of spiritual endeavour, the merger, the *layavastha*, you see, that not only do I become him and become complete, he becomes me and completes that thing.

And I want to conclude this talk by giving you a beautiful story. You know the divine story of Radha and Krishna. I am sure all of you know it. Krishna, the Lord, the *avatara*, had a lover, you see, a girl, a cow maid, Radha, one of sixteen thousand other *gopis* who loved him madly. In addition he had two wives Rukmani and Satyabhama. Now this is not permis-

Stages of Spiritual Evolution

sion to marry twice and to have sixteen thousand girlfriends. It is a divine drama, you see, where according to the Hindu tradition the *sanatana dharma* tradition, every *jivatma*, the embodied soul, is the lover of the Ultimate. It is said in the Hindu tradition that He is the only male, all others are females. Though here we have the bodily differences of the sexes, with God our relationship is always the same; He is the beloved, we are the lovers.

So for the Lord, naturally, all of creation is his lovers. His special lovers were the sixteen thousand and, of them, the most special was this girl Radha. Today for Krishna, he is known as Radha Krishna, you see, Radha comes first. Though we say, men first, in the Indian social life, the woman always comes first in the Hindu household. She is called the *gruhalakshmi*, the wealth of the family, the abundance of the family, the, what shall we say, *kalyana*. As I told Kalyani, the one who brings bliss, cheer, happiness, light, illumination, all this is embodied in the female principle. So he is not Krishna Radha, he is Radha Krishna, you see.

And it was a divine love affair and subsequently, eventually, when he had to leave Vrindavan and go away to Dwaraka to take up his other work, he gave her his flute. That was all that she got out of him, his flute, you know, the wooden bamboo flute in India. And she was, I mean, totally lost in his love and in his remembrance and she was sitting just murmuring his name, you know, "Krishna, Krishna, Krishna." And it is said that this constant remembrance of the Lord made her become him. She became Krishna, and she started murmuring, but the murmur changed to "Radha, Radha, Radha"! Here is a girl murmuring her own name. Anybody who saw her would have thought she was stupid, foolish, you know. "What is this?! She is saying she loves Krishna and she is murmuring her own name." But this was the inner transformation, miraculously achieved by constant remembrance and a total all-consuming love. "Krishna, Krishna, Krishna," you see, and she became Krishna, and now as Krishna she starts saying "Radha! Radha!" So who is loving whom? Who is the lover? Who is the beloved?

You know, that is the miracle of love. Not something which you can grasp, and avariciously seek and maul, you know. That is stupid, that is animal, that is why it is called carnal love, very correctly. In the real love, who is the beloved? Who is the lover? And when that love is finally united together in one grand culmination, you know, of oneness by mergence each into the other, the lover is gone, the beloved is gone, even loving is gone. Then comes that unified unity of existence which knows nothing, not even its own identity, not even its own existence. Now we are at the goal.

Thank you.

6

Faith

West Point, USA
Wednesday, September 28, 1988

People are always asking me whether the seminar has been successfully concluded. I do not think we should look at it in those terms. A seminar can be successful in the conventional way but a total failure if we do not work after that. Or it can be a failure in the conventional sense that everybody goes back angry, frustrated, but willing to work. And then it is a success. So the success or failure of these seminars depends on you. And it is a long term, incremental thing.

So I prefer to say, as I said the other day, that these things must be effective. Success is in being effective. There can be no success without the right effect being inherited from our work. Work gives! Where there is no work, there is nothing. And if we work, the success is there. It has to be there. I say this on the conviction that work, even wrongly done, teaches us something, and is therefore effective. Provided we have the common sense attitude to learn from mistakes and the awareness not to repeat them, every mistake helps us. Therefore, I, for one, am not afraid of making mistakes.

I remember Babuji's letter to me, one of his last letters, where he says, "I have made many mistakes, mistakes and mistakes." And then there is a hyphen and he says, "no mistakes, they are hooting on their own." [he chuckles] It was typically his language, the real meaning of which, I suppose, only he knows. But the attitude is evident there: we should not be bogged down by mistakes. Nor should we be elated by

West Point

success. We move on. And if these seminars help you to keep moving, I think then these seminars have achieved some purpose. I personally believe that all these seminars are achieving something because otherwise we would not be here. Therefore, I wish you all joy of this work. You see, let us not do this work like work. It must be something which we cannot help doing. It must be something which we have to do, which must be our existence. When we separate work from our existence and say, "I have work to do," or "I have to study," then I and my work are separate, I and my study are separate. Therefore, we suffer because where there should be one, there are two. We should not even be conscious we are working. And when there are no abhyasis we should feel a sense of isolation, loneliness, and long for company, that is what is called satsangh, you see.

So I wish that such a situation will develop in all your lives, and that service will become a joy, and the absence of the opportunity to serve will become a desolation. Then only can we be said to be true preceptors. Until then we are like any other worker, you see, going about a day's drudgery, trying to earn something from it, remaining beggars. I do not think that is what we intended when we took on this job, nor what Babuji expected of us. Because as somebody quoted, I think it was one of the speakers yesterday, Babuji does not make slaves but he makes masters. And masters do not whine and suffer. They go around making masters. So, that is your job too.

Before you can make a master you cannot be a master. Isn't it? It is like motherhood, you see. You are a mother only when you have a child. And the thing is simultaneous. You do not become a mother first and then produce a child. So in that sense, one who can produce a master alone is a master. And we have to develop the ability, the capacity, the willingness, and then you will find one day you have sort of slipped into that situation. You are still not conscious that the Master has

Faith

produced a Master in you, but you are able to produce masters and therefore one has to conclude, you see. It is as if you put something in one of these microwave ovens. Normally we do not expect anything to boil or be heated up without a fire. But here you put it on and it beeps a couple of times; and fortunately it does not open the door and push the thing out. [he chuckles] It might! There might be something soon like that [he chuckles], a hot potato thrown in your face.

But you see, that is the way we have to look at our work, with laughter, with joy. "Yes, this is my destiny. This is what I have come here for. This is what my Master has created me for." Otherwise, we are like tools. It is as if an axe would whine and weep, "Oh my wonderful smooth, shining edge. It is being blunted. It is being soiled." And when he grinds the tool again, "Oh, I am being rubbed against a grindstone. Look at the sparks flying from me. I am hot, I am cold, I am this, I am that." We become whiners. But that is no use. We have to go ahead with a sense of purpose — not **our** purpose. A preceptor is true to himself and to the Master when his purpose becomes the purpose of those whom he is supposed to serve. Their lives must become your primary concern; their health is your primary concern, not yours; their upliftment becomes your primary concern, not your own. If you are able to achieve that state of being that, "It does not matter what happens to me so long as I can push a few of these people up," then this miracle can be possible that all are masters, otherwise, it is just a name, or a word in a book.

And then we have all these confabulations, confusions. How many Masters can there be? Can there be only one Master? Should there be a living Master? Well, if there is not a living Master, what will there be, a dead Master? I do not know what people imagine, you see. What would you do with a dead Master? If you have a Master, he must be a living Master,

West Point

in any form, under any name. The message of Christianity, which has been distorted, is the same, you see. Christ said, "I will come again," And we are waiting for that fellow with a beard and, you know, all ready to be crucified all over again, when he will once more say, "I will come again." And the story repeats endlessly, like a cracked gramophone record: "I will come again, I will come again, I will come again, I will come again."

So let us not anguish ourselves or agonize ourselves with these problems by using the intellect. It is like pointing to the photograph. Suppose a woman should point to a photograph and say, "This is my dead husband." It is ridiculous, you see. "He is my husband. He is dead," you see, that is a different story. But you cannot have a dead husband. The husband is dead — true; but he is not, "my dead husband", you see. It is like that famous statement in the British monarchy, you see, when a king dies, the proclamation is made, "The king is dead. Long live the king!" [laughter] Yes! Because one king is dead, the next king is alive. The monarchy cannot be without an incumbent on the throne. He may not have been crowned yet, but he is there. So, "The king is dead. Long live the king!" It looks superficial, ridiculous, laughable, but it is true.

I remember my Master once told me, you see, "Like a state cannot exist without a head, the Mission cannot exist without a head." And, I mean, this is outside the scope of this seminar, but nevertheless there are people who are still agitated with these problems, confusions. His instruction to me was that, "Whenever I pass away, at that moment you should announce that you are my successor, and take over the job, because there cannot be a gap in this matter. There can be no gap in this hierarchy." Like that also, in the preceptor's work, can you be a preceptor only during the time of meditation, or giving a sitting to somebody, and then you are Billy or James or

Faith

whatever you are? It is not only a twenty-four hour job, it is a lifetime involvement in the Master's work. It is as if a potato is a potato till you pluck it out of the ground but the moment you put it in the water to boil it just evaporates away because it does not want to be boiled.

So what is the use of a preceptor who is happy when there is no work, there are only seminars, and peaches and cream, and pizza in the evening, and a nice certificate to hang on the wall? It is not enough, you see. A preceptor is other than these things. He is or she is what they do not appear to be. They are their work, they are their involvement, they are their dedication, they are their integrity to their purpose which they have accepted. Without these they are only other human beings pretending to be preceptors.

So, you see, we need a sense of dedication; we need a sense of purpose; we need a sense of reaffirmation of our sense of purpose; we need to open our eyes to the fact that here is, perhaps, one of the grandest opportunities ever given to us to serve others and thereby to serve ourselves. And if we miss the boat, for any consideration whatever, I do not think there can be any consideration which can interfere in this grand performance, uninterrupted performance, dedicated performance of our duties to ourselves. After all, it is your duty to yourself. When you give a sitting to someone you are serving yourself. As I have repeated so many times, Babuji said, "Even the best preceptor, when he gives transmission, he transmits only eighty percent of what he receives." The twenty percent is held back. And he said, "Where else can you get a twenty percent commission? This is the best business in the world."

But we think it is a chore, we think it interferes with childcare, with the, I do not know, the microwave oven has been switched on, or we are expecting a phone call. So we have no time to meditate, we have even less time for others, and we continue this rather unfortunate parody of a preceptor's existence: not serving others, therefore not serving ourselves. Then, you see, all the tears in the world are not going to be useful to us. I dare say tears are only a sign of weakness, you see, at any stage of life.

So we should try to see that we live the dedication which we have accepted. That we try to fulfill the responsibilities which are implied in our acceptance of the preceptor's job. And that most importantly we must understand, you see, with our heart, that this is the highest opportunity of serving ourselves. It is coming through somebody else, you see, my service to myself has to come through somebody else. Like I have to see my face reflected in a mirror; I have to eat something to fill my stomach so that I may exist. The burden is on the stomach, but I exist.

So when we understand this circularity, you see, of my service coming back to me through another person, or other persons, then perhaps our eyes will be opened to this most magnificent of all opportunities, and our work must become a magnificent obsession with us. I do not think anything short of an obsession with this work will suffice. Interest is not enough, dedication is not enough. It must be an obsession, you see, the grand obsession, the great obsession, call it what you like. Then it is possible that Master's hope that he produces or creates masters can be fulfilled. Otherwise, we remain preceptors at several levels of achievement, of several levels of effort, some convinced, some unconvinced, some doing, some not doing so much. So this must be the thing that we should understand, you see, and this we can understand only when we work. And we find this miraculous possibility that we have no time to meditate, we have no time to do the cleaning, yet we are progressing.

Faith

It was in Grace Kimball's house in Lakewood Ohio in 1972, you see, one morning Babuji called me and said, "You need not meditate any more." I said, "How is that possible? It is a lifelong process." He said, "Not for you. Lalaji has said that you need not meditate any more, but there is one condition." I knew there was [laughter] [he laughs] a string attached, you see, but anyway, the Master was the Master. So I said, "What is it?" He said, "The time you shall thus save must be given to the Mission's work." Now that was very simple, you see. We do one hour's meditation. I was prepared to give him one hour's work. [laughter] [he laughs] But that was the first footstep into the, what do you call it, the quicksands of spirituality. But it is a happy quicksand. I have never regretted it. I go deeper and deeper into it. And I find that the quicksand is, after all, nothing but the vortex of time, which is drawing you into eternity. And why should we be afraid of that? Whether you like it or not you are going there one day. Let us go with happiness, with a smile, with cheerfulness, and doing something, you see.

So you see this conclusion is inescapable. And in future seminars, I hope we will be able to see the reinforcement of this attitude in the preceptors. As I said in Courmettes, and as I repeat now, success is not the criterion. There can be no success without effort, and there can be no effort without dedication. There can be no dedication without right understanding of the purpose of the work. And when you understand that the purpose of your work is yourself, and the ennoblement and the glorification of yourself up to the highest limits open to us, then surely you will not only be tempted to work, you will be compelled to work, you will be forced to work, you cannot rest without working, you see. It is that restlessness of which Babuji spoke for the abhyasi, which restlessness we must duplicate in our lives as preceptors. And that restlessness will lead us to the goal.

So please think over these things. Do your work without thinking of whether your reading is right or wrong. It does not matter. What matters is the reading. You must realise that famous parallel from the sports: what matters is participation, not the winning. He who never participates because he is afraid to lose, remains at home. But a sportsman is a sportsman, you see. It takes many people to have a race. Can you have just one man running an Olympic event and being given the gold medal? They would not give it to him. They cannot say, "There is only one participant in this event. And even if he completes the mile in seventeen and a half minutes, we award him the gold medal." That is not the way it is done, you see. There have to be many participants. They have to run as if their lives depended upon it. And the man who was prepared to lose his life came out first. He found a second wind, he found a third wind, and he found the ultimate wind perhaps, having no wind, yet it was there.

So, if that is the attitude for a mere gold medal and your name in the newspaper, should we not try to, in some way, parallel that effort here too. That is all we seek, that is all we ask for. That is all you must demand from yourself. It is not the Master's work to keep pulling preceptors up as if they were truant students in a classroom. Preceptors, I think, merit much more than that. But that merit they have to earn, you see, by their work and by their dedication. Then the Master must be able to say, "Without him or without her my work will suffer." Otherwise, like Babuji used to say, "There are so many of them. What is the use?"

I remember in Delhi when he was speaking, I think, in 1980, before going to Denmark, he said, "I have worked single-handed, and the result is before you all to see." It was a shaming statement for all of us. Many people were only praising Babuji. "Look at him, you see. One man, frail man, old man, thin man,"

Faith

all these things, "He has done so much." The more they praised, the more I felt ashamed. They had not understood Babuji's remark or its thrust. He did not say it for himself to be praised, that, "I am doing this, and I have done this alone, and look at the result." It was not for him that he wanted us to clap and say, "What a wonderful old person you are." He wanted us to feel ashamed, saying, "I have made so many of you and yet I am alone."

You see, you all know this loneliness when you are married, when you have children, and yet at home you feel totally lonely. Why? You are surrounded by people and you are lonely. You are in a big apartment complex with seven hundred and twenty apartments, two thousand and six hundred people in the building and yet you are lonely. So, what was his loneliness? His loneliness was that he created people who were supposed to support his work, not help, **support,** and they just relaxed, and assumed that being a preceptor was good enough. We are not bricks, that being a brick in the wall we do some work without doing anything. That is inanimate matter. It rests. It is there, and by being there it serves. We are required to do something. Otherwise, we are like a car into which you get and the engine does not start, yet you play around with the gears, press the accelerator pedal and pretend you are moving.

So you see, Master's, I think it was his anguish of that moment, his realisation that all that he had done over the past thirty-five years, the hundreds of preceptors he had made (they were there in name, certificates had been issued), but he had still to do all the work. I do not think he was complaining. Otherwise he would have bluntly said, "You fellows have let me down." He did not say that. He said it with a sense of anguish, "How much I have expected of you, not for my sake, but for your sake. How much you could have done, not for me, but for yourself. You have made me do it, and therefore robbed yourself of the fruit of that labour. Because when I do something the fruit of it accrues only to me. And even though I wish to give it to you, I cannot give it to you because the law of work and reward is absolute." I think that was his main thrust. Being a preceptor is not enough. Doing what a preceptor has to do, then becoming what a preceptor has to become, because after all a preceptor is only a name, we have to become something now.

So these are the small lessons that we have to learn from the words of the Master, from his work. Try to see what he did in it, what he did it for. Was it only because he had promised Lalaji that he would carry on his work? I mean, he could have easily resiled from that promise. "What is the need to abide by the promise? Lalaji has gone. Let me sit back and relax." He need not have killed himself until he died. Every moment he was working. And we were all very pleased, we were always joking, laughing, "What a wonderful old Master we have! You see, he does not rest even a moment. He is always occupied with us. How wonderful **we** are!"

So that was the fault, that is still the fault. Only thing we can pray is that it should not be the fault in the future. And if this attitude, again, you couple with the other thing, that when we work, we work for ourselves, apparently we are serving others, but we are serving ourselves. It is the same in all activities. You are an architect, you build a house for somebody; in serving him, you also line your coffers. You are a cook, you cook for somebody else and sell the food; in serving him, you also line your own pockets. Why do we work, even for a wage? We would not work unless we got something out of it. In some enterprises you get a lot out of it, in some you think you do not get anything out of it. Preceptors think they do not get anything at all, but that is a mistake. We get the highest possible reward of anything, because we get Him.

Faith

I do not think I have to say much more, except to wish you all the joy of the spiritual life, and the glories of a spiritual existence, and hope that you will all savour it in your own personal experience.

Thank you.

II

Questions and Answers

7

Sunday, July 10, 1988

Q: In the text *Towards Infinity*, Babuji mentions, he is talking about sub-points. Sometimes he uses the word point and sometimes sub-point. I think it is point three or four, he says, "and then we move to the next sub-point."

PR: Well, that is in the description. He has himself said there are an infinite number of points in the system. We are only describing the major points, you see. Like between here and Lyon there are an infinite number of places, some with names, many without names. Isn't it? I mean, a place is a place, you only name towns and villages, hamlets. What about all the pieces of land which you do not name? So in that way, or in an inch, you say one-tenth of an inch, one-hundredth; but there could be one-thousandth, and if you divided it into a million? What is your general impression of today? I mean the talk. No comments. Do you think it is serving a purpose or not?

Q: It is serving the purpose that you brought out this morning, that we should learn to read the condition at the point, if it is for our benefit.

PR: Of course, it is not for your benefit directly. It is for your benefit in that you will be able to better do the work you have taken up.

Q: The work?

PR: All capacity is like that, you see. For instance, if you are learning carpentry and you become a master carpenter, of course you earn more money, but it is to serve the clients better, you know, to give better products, better goods, "deliver the goods" as we say. All capacity is to serve. The incremental achievement that you get for your personal needs is incidental. That it has been converted as something to fulfil ourselves is a peculiar inversion of Occidental culture. What is your opinion?

This exercise is to enable me to sort of, you know, change, to suit your needs. Because I am not doing this for myself, obviously. You know, I do not need these lectures and these exercises. I have to learn from my Master, I do not learn from myself. I am trying to pass on to you something, you know, which will help you in your work. Because I sincerely hope that all of you are serious about this work of the preceptor, and I know that much of the frustration is because you are not able to do what you would like to do. Not for want of intention, or intent, but for lack of the ability to do so. And not for lack of the real ability, but an imagined lack. Because, as I tried to point out this morning, we see, and we note what we see. But when you start with a preconception of trying to see something, you may not find it.

You know, I was thinking this afternoon, I was alone in my room, there are two ways of training perception. You know these jumble lines with numbers, and you have to trace the outline of a bird or something, you know, find the peacock in the above dotted area. Then you are trying to look for something in a maze, or a jumble of things. The other is: find what there is here in this. And then you can see various pictures, for instance like the Rorschach test, you know, where the imagination comes into play. Now here, we are doing neither. We are looking to see what there is. Neither to find something which we think is there, nor to find something which somebody else says is there, but to look. And one single rule Babuji told me, "Anything black, remove! Anything light, let it stay." So this principle is so utterly easy, and you know, I should think even children should be able to do it.

Sunday, July 10, 1988

Now, what is the difficulty? I experienced the difficulty for several years, you see. Now, we all have certain cultural implantations. For instance if you talk of God to a Hindu, he thinks of a god with four arms, multiple legs, you know, weapons in each. It is his training. If he sees God in his experience, he sees God in that form. A Christian sees Christ. A Buddhist sees Buddha. It is not that Buddha appeared; it is your vision manifesting itself in a form in which you can recognize it. You understand? That is why I once said that if a cow saw God, it would see it as a big, enormously big, bull. It could not see God in an anthropomorphic form. Obviously not! So, we are trained, culturally, socially, by virtue of our tradition, heritage, to see certain things in certain ways. Here we have to learn to see reality. So it is very necessary to forget all this accumulation that we have gathered; and to perceive reality as such. This is the problem. It is not that we are not seeing. We are expecting to see something.

Like, you know, you take a child to a zoo, it has never seen an elephant before, and at every cage or every enclosure it says, "Daddy, is this the elephant?" You say, "No darling, this is a bull, this is a cow, that is a deer. This is a peacock, you know, it has wings, it flies, how could it be an animal?" So, you teach it by process of elimination until you come to the elephant. By that time the child is generally too tired and has gone to sleep. [laughter] This happens to us too, you see. So, to see reality means uncluttering your mind of all preconceptions, notions, and making it, you know, like a beam of a torch, like a flashlight, point it where you will, it only shows what there is. Now, when you are looking with a flashlight for a ring which you have lost, when you are searching for something specific, you may not find it, you may find it. But if the Master says, "Take the flashlight, point it there and tell me what you see!" I mean, to me it appears ridiculously simple! But suppose you start thinking, "What does the Master want me to find there?" Then we get into trouble. So, the whole purpose of this training is to clear the mind of all the fog, of all cloud, and make us see what there is, and not what we want to see, or what we expect to see. And then comes the next step, you know, of cleaning. That we shall tackle later.

Q: Then it may be a projection?

PR: No, no, without projection. Why? If I say there is an elephant here, without telling you where it is, you have to find the elephant. But if I tell you, "There is an animal here, please go and see what it is," then you do not know what it is and you have to really look hard. It may be a tiger, it may be an antelope, it may just be a cat, or a person like me, [laughter] an animal. Now, I tell you, you have to find and see! And once you know what to look for, it is there. So first you look for yourself, then you compare it. If you are right, well, there is nothing more to be said. It is very good. You can give yourself a pat on the back because I will not be available. [he laughs] But if it does not tally, and if you would like to check again, request that abhyasi to come and sit for a few minutes and check. It is a simple way.

Q: The question of the level of approach; do you think...

PR: That is a little premature. It needs more concentration. It is also difficult. But at the level of the abhyasi you are tackling that, too, is not difficult. Suppose you have a loooong [he emphasizes long] stairway going up and I tell you to count the number of stairs, it may be infinite; but if I ask you, "How many stairs are here?" you would just look and say, "Twenty-two." So, there you have to be able to locate, because as they go up, receding into the distance, you can hardly distinguish one stair from the other. And in the very high regions, for instance, central region, Babuji said it is almost impossible. And he used to tell me to note down in my diary where I am. He would read

Sunday, July 10, 1988

and then say, "Note it." I said, "Why should I note it?" He said, "Because if I have to locate you again, it requires tremendous concentration of which I am not capable, and I do not wish to waste energy on it." You know how difficult it is sometimes to locate a plane. The noise indicates its presence here; it is actually there. You know? So we have to learn to position things, and that is a little more tricky. But in the region of the heart there is no problem. And I can assure you that all of them are in the heart region. So you can start looking again.

Q: What is the value of it?

PR: Value?

Q: The value of knowing a person's approach.

PR: If you are going to put two pieces of wood together and screw them, you know, you have to know where to put the screw. Isn't it? And drill a hole there. Not drill a hole anywhere and put a screw anywhere and then you find the two pieces hanging apart. So, the deeper you go into the work, you have to become more and more refined in your approach. What is the difference between the preceptor and the Master? It is only the refinement, isn't it? What is the difference between pure gold and gold ore? It is only the refinement, or the dross is taken out. What is the difference between man and God? As Babuji said, "This is gross, that is totally subtle." What does it mean? That when all the grossness is removed, subtlety is there! You do not create subtlety; you remove grossness.

8

Tuesday, July 12, 1988

PR: Suppose your higher point is gross, the tendency is stronger. You know, this is why you have to read. When I wrote in one case: first and third points are gross, second point is illuminated; the grossness at the third point assumes more potency, you see. For example, a brick on the ground cannot hurt anybody. If I throw it from here, it can crack your skull, if I throw it from there [pointing upwards] it can kill you. The brick is the same. Isn't it? It has more potential energy by being at a higher level.

Q: Does that mean that you say some grossness, for example at the third point, is a specific tendency?

PR: No, no.

Q: It is a misunderstanding.

PR: More potency in that situation than in a lower point. Therefore it is dangerous when grossness is in the higher regions.

Q: Can a new abhyasi be gross throughout? You know what I mean?

PR: Yes, it is possible. Generally they are, at the beginning. But when you do the cleaning you will find that sometimes the higher regions are bright and the lower regions continue to be gross. Sometimes you will find the contrary. The lower regions get quickly cleaned, the higher regions are difficult to clean, precisely because it is more subtle. You know, it is like removing smoke from a room. Cigarette butts you can sweep out. What do you do with the smoke? You have to open all your windows, put a blower and things like that. The subtler the grossness, the more difficult it is to remove. I have to finally give another talk on cleaning, maybe, because it is the most important thing in Sahaj Marg. If you read my first book, *India in the West*, you will find all the lectures I gave in Europe were basically devoted to cleaning, you see. Babuji said, "Speak about cleaning, the importance of cleaning." It is most important.

Q: Is that pattern of grossness just from samskara?

PR: Yes. There is nothing else. The reason for existence is samskara. I mean in this temporary existence, not in eternal existence. Samskara brings you into this world. Remove samskara and you go into the brighter world.

Q: Isn't there also this business of samskara and tendencies.

PR: Tendency relates to behaviour. You know, like we say, he has a tendency to be upset. What creates the tendency is the grossness. You know, like some children are prone to measles. They do not catch cold and things, but expose them to measles and they are sick. The doctors call it proneness to a disease. Why? Because in your organism you are susceptible, as they say, to that particular disease. Exposed to that, you succumb. To anything else you are immune. That is why you introduce antibodies by way of vaccination and things like that, and create a disease, and then create immunity to it within the system itself. But here there is no such automatic system, you know. And now what happens. A man gets angry; he gets, let us say, an impression, a big impression. This impression colours his next activity, and it comes again without his knowing. The impression is made stronger. The third time he erupts. Like I told you the humorous example of my father, who used to be very irritable. Babuji told him, "I am telling you, Rajagopalachari, you must remove this irritation." "NO! NO! Where is my irritation!?!" says my father. "What is this?"

Tuesday, July 12, 1988

Babuji asked him. Everybody laughed. That comes to the stage where you are what you are without your even knowing what you are.

Q: Was this even though he was already put in the central region?

PR: Yes, but why? Even then the tendency can still be there.

Q: So you said there is the grossness, and from the grossness we get that tendency.

PR: And the tendency creates further grossness. You are forgetting that. You see, like a thought creates activity, activity creates the grossness, that grossness enforces the fault again, which is a tendency, and the activity is repeated, because it is linked with that thing.

Q: Yes. Which means, that once when you move a person to high levels, you are supposed to clean the heart region, and clean the grossness.

PR: Yes, but if you re-create everyday the grossness...

Q: Which means then you do not clean the tendency entirely?

PR: It is not possible. Tendency becomes a behavioristic thing, a pattern. Now, it is no longer dependent on your grossness. That is why it is easier to train children than grown-ups.

Q: This is why there is so much insistence on controlling our behaviour?

PR: Exactly.

Q: This is what I found out.

PR: No, no. This is what Babuji said, "Spirituality is my business. Character formation is your responsibility."

Q: So, we can lose the tendencies if we co-operate?

PR: Yes. You can lose it even without losing the grossness. It is possible. But the grossness will still impede your progress.

But that is the Master's business, you see. "At least we can co-operate to the extent that we do not re-create," that is what Babuji said, "I keep removing and you keep creating."

Q: You gave a beautiful image about that. Samskara is like the water of the river and tendencies are the bed.

PR: The river bed. Not tendency, that it creates like that, you see. And when water falls again, it flows through that channel. So it becomes the tendency. So Babuji said, "We must remove the river bed." People dry up the river, but they forget the bed is still there. And when again water comes it will only flow the same way. That is why we repeat our behaviour in the same fashion. However much we like to change, we are not able to change, because that bed through which it flows has not been leveled out. It is like a footpath. People walking on the same way, because it is the easiest way. Your foot finds itself naturally there, and you trace a footpath. The grass does not grow any more there.

Q: Which also shows that it is very difficult to change our behaviour, since there is that river bed.

PR: Please, that is no excuse. [laughter] If you can co-operate, you see, suppose rain water does not fall, the river bed will not effect you. Now what is that rain which is falling? You are being exposed to the outer world. If you are in constant remembrance, there is no problem.

Ultimately, as I have been telling you so many times, constant remembrance is the single cure for everything. Then you cannot form any impression. If you are thinking of the Master and something is going on, even a bloody murder, it will not affect you. Normally, if you see someone being hacked to death, you know, you cannot sleep. And sometimes for months you cannot sleep, and you even would not like to go to that place. But if you are in the remembrance of the Master, it

Tuesday, July 12, 1988

is just another scene. It does not affect you. I may not be able to cover everything in this session. Now, I thought, what am I going to do, now I think time is not enough.

Q: Is it possible to ascribe any period of time, any length of time for, let us say, in the case of a person who is ridden with tendencies and samskaras and the person starts constant remembrance, and does not leave it? How long will it take?

PR: One week.

Q: To get that person rid of all the tendencies?

PR: No, no. It is rid. The moment you are in constant remembrance, the tendency is gone. The two cannot exist side by side. It is only when we slip out of remembrance that this world grasps us. It is like a man, you know, as long as he is in the train, he is not on the ground. The moment he is on the ground, he is not in the train. He cannot be in both. So slip out of remembrance, this world catches you. Get into remembrance, this world loses its hold. Absolutely!

Q: That is very important.

Q: I had the impression that there are times when I was not concentrating, and then I was. I felt that some tendencies had left, and then later on that remembrance disappeared, and then I found those tendencies again.

PR: Yes. That is what I am telling you.

Q: In that case I was not in constant remembrance.

PR: No, no. When you were in remembrance, the tendency was not there. That is what I have told you. When you come back out of remembrance, the tendency is there because the grossness is there. Now, for a man who is clean and in constant remembrance, nothing can happen. What do we do? Either we are slipping in or out of remembrance, which is no longer constant remembrance, and we are subjected to this world.

Courmettes

When we are here, we are subjected to this, the law of gravitation, let us say. When we are there, we are pulled up. We are like a yo-yo, you know, moving up and down. And in the higher-up people, they are fully clean, but they are not in remembrance. See, the two have to go together. Absolutely. Clean system and constant remembrance. If the two are there, instant saint.

Q: When I am in remembrance, then I also forget any idea of progress and all that, not only tendencies from the lower but also from everything.

PR: Why should we remember progress? We should remember the Master. Progress is immaterial.

Q: Only if you go out, then comes the lower?

PR: That will come in my last talk, all this question of progress and whatnot.

Q: So, these are signs that if you are not in balance...

PR: For the one who is able to be in constant remembrance, he is the Master at that moment. For him, he can do anything. Because it is not his activity any more. I told somebody to remind me to tell a story and they forgot.

Q: Yes, I remember.

PR: About constant remembrance. But why did not you tell me.

Q: Maybe because it was not the right time.

PR: I told you to remind me. I did not ask you to remind me at the right time. [laughter]

Q: Not at me. I was there sleeping and you asked to this gentleman.

Q: Yes.

PR: Ah, you did not remind me. At least you remember that I told you. [laughter]

Tuesday, July 12, 1988

Q: Chariji, I am only a watcher.

PR: No, no. But suppose, you see, if I am telling Otto, "Please, if there is a fire, telephone the fire department," [he laughs] and you say, "I am only a watcher. You told Otto and he did not telephone," what can I do, the house is burnt.

Q: We can remind you tonight.

PR: No, no. I want to speak there so that everybody will hear. It is a most beautiful and a very important story. This time, at least you remind me, even if you are the watcher. [laughter]

Q: (inaudible) the tendencies and the constant remembrance. I think it is very essential. If you would be so kind.

PR: I will be covering all that, you know, "Be so kind," [laughter] but I have so much to say, and I am nervous, and you know I get negative feedback which puts me off.

Q: Yes. Because really there was a lot of positive feedback.

Q: Do you mean to say that you never get any positive feedback? You simply give more importance to the negative feedback than to the positive.

PR: You see, I will tell you, once there was a problem in India. A very big problem affecting senior people, their code of conduct, so many things. We were in Madurai. Now, I was nervous about telling this to Babuji, lest he should think I was carrying tales. So I asked him, "Babuji, there are certain things going on. Should I tell you or not?" He said, "What things?" I said, "If I tell you, I have told you what I want to tell you."

Babuji said, "General rule. Good things you do not have to tell me. I do not have to know it. A doctor does not have to tell me I am healthy. Only when I am sick, he has to tell me. Similarly, if anything goes wrong, it is your duty to tell me. So, inevitably, we get only the negatives. But at the same time it affects. It is like the wife who says, "If there is anything wrong with the cooking today please tell me." And you say, "Well, there darling." and she says, "So!" [laughter] and she throws the saucepan in your face. [he laughs] [laughter] What to do? It happens like that. You know, we have to...

Q: I heard lots of people who were very interested in what you said. They appreciated it very much.

PR: Well, I hope so.

Q: But you always get people who are not happy whatever you do or say.

PR: You know, all these weeks people were free to come, they did not come. This one week when you say nobody can come, everybody wants to come. I had even a reference today, that, "Oh, such and such a person is only here. Poor woman, she is suffering. She knew it was only for preceptors, but having come she expected..." you know. What can I do?

Q: It is always the same thing. For children, if you tell them, "You should not smoke. You must not smoke," the only thing they want to do is to smoke.

PR: Yes, there is this temptation to do what you should not do. Always! And they think something special is going on. And they want to sit in this sitting. You know, it can be destructive sometimes.

Shri Ishwar Sahai, you know, Master's companion in those days, was a blundering bear-like person. He would blunder around. He would hit the chair, throw a couple of cups on the floor, but he was always with Babuji twenty-four hours a day, for many years. Now it seems Babuji was giving a sitting to Kasturi and he walked through between them. Babuji told him, "Do not walk between us because it can be dangerous." First of all, it is not etiquette, you see. Two or three times this happened. He never obeyed. Then Babuji's guru-brother

Tuesday, July 12, 1988

Pandit Rameshwar Prasad told Babuji, "You leave him to me. [laughter] I will set him right." So one day he was giving transmission to Kasturi. Shri Ishwar Sahai came. He said, "Do not pass between us, it can be harmful." He said, "No, no. Babuji is transmitting; every time I go. Nothing happens." Pandit Rameshwar Prasad started the sitting. Shri Ishwar Sahai went through. He was thrown to the wall five metres away, like a football, PATANG [he makes this sound]. [laughter] So Pandit Rameshwar Prasad, very innocently asked, "What is happening?" [laughter] That man, poor man, he got up with bruises and sores, and asked, "How did this happen?" Panditji asked, "Oh, it happened? Oh, no! I told you for a joke, but it has happened."

Q: Did he push him?

PR: No, no, transmission, only transmission, you see. Babuji was very soft. People came, you know, "No, no, Babuji, what can you do?" He said, "Oh, I am telling you, you know, it is very good for you." And he said, "Oh, it is very good?", and he goes away. So Pandit Rameshwar Prasad used to tell Babuji, "*Bhai saheb* (elder brother), you are not fit for this work. Why do these people come and bother you? Leave them to me." And he would give them such a transmission that they could not get up and walk. [laughter] You know, they would be staggering like drunkards. And he used to knock down monkeys from the wall with transmission. And the monkey fell. Rameshwar Prasadji — about him Babuji used to tell so many stories. He said, "You know, you should not do this. Lalaji does not like it." Panditji said, "Brother, your way is your way. My way is my way." [laughter]

Q: Is that the one with the tiger?

PR: Yes. He was the one who came riding on a tiger in Sitapur. And he asked Babuji, "How many abhyasis have you got? You

Courmettes

are slaving all your life — twenty-seven people. What is this? You know, kindness, love? Yes, keep it in your heart; but give them the transmission in such a way that they cannot go home again." In 1972 Babuji told me, after our European trip, he said, "I am very sorry Rameshwar Prasad is not here." I said, "Why today?" He said, "You are exactly like him. [laughter] Today he would have been a happy man if he had seen you." Sometimes it works against.

Q: Are you riding the tiger?

PR: Oh, I am riding a tiger all the time. I have also to give a sitting at 3:30. Not much work.

Q: Did he die old, that man? Was he old when he died?

PR: Pandit Rameshwar Prasad? Same as Babuji's age, I think. But he died much earlier. He may have been a few years older than Babuji. He was a preceptor of Lalaji's. Funny thing is Babuji was never a preceptor in Lalaji's time.

Q: He died long ago?

PR: Oh, he died long ago. In 1948 maybe. You know, he was there when the Mission was established. Must have been a few years later, 1952, 1953. I think he was also alive when Babuji's wife passed away — 1953 that was. So he must have died in 1955 or 1956.

Q: And he accepted Babuji as the representative of Lalaji?

PR: Yes, yes. He was the only man who accepted him, of all of Lalaji's disciples.

Q: I thought there were three or four of his disciples?

PR: They came subsequently. The man who accepted him implicitly, without question, was Pandit Rameshwar Prasad.

Q: Who wrote that song in Babuji's memory?

Tuesday, July 12, 1988

PR: Aftabe Marfat. Oh, there were people who tried to poison Babuji — Lalaji's disciples. And Rameshwar Prasad used to eat first and then feed him.

Q: Are there still some left over from this split-off group?

PR: From Lalaji's time? Yes, there are seven or eight groups.

Q: Seven or eight groups?

PR: Yes, yes. There are so many people. They are publishing books. They are using the name *Ram Chandra Mission* now. Because we are very successful, you see, and known worldwide, they are using the same name; writing to the people we write to. What can you do? They say that imitation is a form of praise of the original. So whenever they imitate we have to be happy. So we must be something, you know, that they choose to imitate us.

Q: Chari, are you going to talk about how far we should pursue people who have left. You know, that took sittings long ago?

PR: Well, in a human way, it is our duty, you know. I said today, at that moment, you know, the crisis comes.

Q: No. But, I mean, from years ago.

PR: Yes. Why not? When you think of them, it means there is something in Nature which prompted that thought. Try what you can. It does not mean you have to go out of the way, and stand there, and hold a flag, you know.

Q: You know Ramakrishnan. He wrote to me with this list of about twenty people from 1972: first name, try to find this guy and tell him, you know, that Chari is going to be in Atlanta. There was this whole list.

PR: But last time he did it one couple did come.

Q: Yeah, yeah. I am just saying that it is going to be a difficult job tracing these people.

PR: No, no. You do not have to go that far. But when a thought comes of someone, Babuji used to tell me, you know, I told him once, sitting at night sometimes in my bed, suddenly I remembered some persons. I said, "Does it have any significance?" He said, "You are a preceptor. Just transmit for a few seconds. It has some meaning. There is a call from them, you see."

Q: Transmit or clean?

PR: I used to transmit. He told me to transmit. Because cleaning takes more time, you know. It is a call for help. It is like a man who has fallen down a ditch. You do not send him down flashlights and transistor radios. You pull him out first. So I used to do it. Then once, one of our preceptors left and I was very upset because he was one person I had introduced, and taken to Babuji and done so much, you know. I asked Babuji what to do. He said, "Well, just have the thought that he is coming back towards the Master. Think that daily he is coming nearer and nearer, but do not connect him with the Master, because then he will get the benefit and he will never come. He will think he is getting it from somewhere." So you have to just keep that gap. And sure enough, after a couple of weeks, that man came grinning from ear to ear. I said, "What happened?" He said, "Oh! Oh! You must have thought I have left the Mission." I said, "No, you told me you were leaving." "No, no, that was just a joke, you see, I was annoyed." All these techniques work. At least they have worked for me. I do not see why they should not work for you.

Q: Is it something which can be used for people who are prejudiced?

PR: For prejudice you have to do cleaning. Because otherwise they will come with the prejudice. What is the use? That is why,

Tuesday, July 12, 1988

you know, this is for people who leave and you want to bring them back. Bring them back and then attend to them.

Q: You said that you want to bring them back. But if you do not really want to, but you do not know. If we think of all the preceptors that have left?

PR: You do not think of them unless you want to think of them in some way, you know. Even if it is a brother you do not like, and you have not seen him for three years, and you suddenly think, "Oh, I will call my brother," you know, and next morning he is there. Now people can argue, "Is it your thought which brought him?" Well, if he thought of you, it could be his thought also. Still, it is the thought.

Q: Is it something we could do with people who have left the Mission because they would not recognize you as the successor?

PR: Shall I tell you how many people have come back, including the South Africans? How have they come back? [laughter] It takes time. The bigger the fish the longer you allow him to play. Otherwise it will break the line, you know. Give it its head. You know, four hours, five hours, the poor thing is swimming as we pull it in. Then it regains its strength and starts swimming all over again. And then you pull it in again. Sometimes you have to do eight hours. Only a fisherman knows. All that patience and the reel, and probably your finger gets cut a little. So you wear gloves. And then when you reel the big fellow in, you know, he's a whopper. They take the longest time.

Q: You should write a fishing guide.

PR: I know many things which I have not done. It is not necessary to do something to know it. This is the first law of wisdom. In the West you believe in experiencing to know about it. We believe it is a fool who will experience when he can know without experiencing. It is like saying, "I want to put my finger in the fire so that I know what burning is like." Nobody does it, you see. A child may do it in its innocence, the first time and, "Waaaaah" it runs. Second time, it will never go near the fire. But when we become adults, we think this fire will not burn. Only that fire burnt me. And he gets burnt a second time, and a third time. And in the next life he comes with a fear of fire. He will not even light a match stick. "No, no, you please light the candle." And you wonder why, you know. Imagine a grown-up fellow, six feet four inches, backwoodsman from Canada. Every time he wants to light a candle, he gives the matchbox to somebody else. "Why don't you light it?" "No, no, you know, I prefer you to light it. I am very clumsy and I can drop the match on the carpet." All sorts of excuses, except the right one. This becomes like that, you know, and it follows you through life.

So that is the danger of doing things which you should not do, knowing they are going to harm you. The harm is multiplied. And when we call this morality, everybody says, "Oh, it is Indian morality." Or it is this or that, you know. Morality is for your benefit. There is no God who is watching to see who is sleeping with whom. What does He care? It is for us. Every time we make a mistake and we repeat it, in the next life you become a man who hates women — a misogynist — and then you have to go to a psychiatrist all over again. "No, no, I am afraid of women." *Pas problem* (no problem). Lie down and give me five hundred francs first." [laughter] All these things result out of past wrong experiences indulged in. An experience which comes by itself, you know, like I stumble and fall without knowing — it cannot harm me. That is experience which tells you, "Don't fall." But a man who climbs a mountain, breaks his leg, goes again, breaks his leg, goes again,

Tuesday, July 12, 1988

breaks his leg — next time he will break his neck. Nature is a harsh teacher, you see. It begins softly.

Q: When one is cleaning there is still something behind it. It is not nothing behind it?

PR: No, no, how can there be nothing? "Nothing comes from nothing. It never could. [he chuckles] Somewhere in my youth or my childhood, I may have done something good," not 'must have'. [he chuckles] Crazy! Isn't it? We must remember my Master's language, "Beyond and beyond."

Q: What is the need for questions?

PR: No need at all. We can say, trying to copy Babuji's way, "That where an answer exists there should be a question." [laughing] He said it the other way around, "Where there is a question, the answer is in itself." So sometimes I think it is like a cat chasing its own tail. Question chasing answer, answer chasing question, you know. [he chuckles] Which comes first? Nobody knows. Really! Because it is not just a play with words. Really, nobody knows whether the question comes first or the answer! Because Babuji has said there can be, in the cause and effect relationship, effects before causes. [he chuckles] Now how is that possible? With your rational mind you cannot make it out, but it is possible.

Q: It is on two levels. You have an effect of a higher level having a cause in the lower. Surely.

PR: Yes, it is an effect which makes a cause which in turn creates the effect which created the cause. You have to ponder over it.

Q: It is like a tendency when the samskara is removed, you know.

PR: And the tendency can remove the samskara, or create the samskara.

Q: Yes, because the tendency, when the samskara is removed, it creates again the samskara.

PR: Yes. These are things which we have to understand with the heart. The intellectual system fails. Because only what is rational, the intellect can understand. What is beyond rationality, how can the intellect understand? Similarly grace, you know. Let us take 'mercy'. You have the president of your South Africa. He can release any prisoner he chooses. There is no law. But the judge cannot release. The judge has to judge and give the sentence. Isn't it? But the president is a politician. He can do what he likes. On Pretoria National Day, "Release all the prisoners." They are released. Nobody can appeal. It is an act of mercy. For mercy, there is no law. There is no justification. Similarly for Divine grace, why has it fallen on this fool and not on me? Who can question grace?

So in spirituality, you see, grace transcends everything. And if you can invite His grace? In fact, all these things we are doing are to invite His grace. Sadhana alone can achieve nothing. As I told you, meditation is only something to clean your mind, regulate it, make it an instrument of revelation. What can you do with it for finding God? Remembrance is to create love. Where is the law that the lover should respond to your love? But all this, you know, like a child when it cries, you rush and take it in your hands. It attracts your attention. Therefore, I think, Christ said, "Be ye as little children." Then your innocence makes Him come down. And that innocence is also a state of dependence. But it does not know its dependence. When we become older we say, "Why should I depend? I am a German. I am a Frenchman. I am a man." All this nonsense comes. And we try to be self-dependent. And then we are finished. So, surrender becomes difficult, you see, progressively. In that innocent state, the child is not surrendering

Tuesday, July 12, 1988

either. Nor does it know it is dependent. But its state attracts. We have to be like that.

Q: Does not innocence mean almost purity? You be innocent of the state of self-awareness.

PR: Innocence means also the lack of the knowledge of purity and dirtiness, of ugliness and beauty, of vice and virtue. Therefore the fall of Adam is construed as a fall into the knowledge of good and evil. And when you are knowledgeable about good and evil, you become bound by the rules of good and evil. An animal does so many things without knowing what it is doing. It cannot be punished. Even human beings, you know, if you are under a mental strain, or you are mentally upset and you do something, you are not given the ultimate punishment. "While of unsound mind, three years." Otherwise you get thirty, or [he demonstrates a beheading]. So it is a state in which you know, and knowing, do it that is punishable.

Q: Considering the discussion on life and taking of life, what is the idea of a soldier?

PR: Well, he is taking life.

Q: Is he allowed to in the spiritual sense?

PR: There comes the concept of duty, you see. Life in what form? You are thinking only of the human. When you hunt deer and bison and elephants, you do not think of it as life. You should not kill anything. But there is a law which says, suppose a child is being attacked by a snake, a poisonous snake, you are allowed to kill the snake to protect the child's life, because it is a higher form of existence. The lower can be sacrificed for the higher. But between human beings, you cannot say immediately, "Blacks are lower, kill the beggars off." They are all human beings. There is no higher and lower within human beings. No, because you are South African, I am pointing this out to you, specifically. That is why it is said, "Dog eats not dog." Isn't it? Yes, there is a famous saying, "Dog eats not dog." Nothing eats its own kind, except the human being who can be a cannibal. Love for the self comes. "Thou cannot love God and mammon." The mammon is the self.

Q: Chariji, are we all in danger?

PR: No, no. Why do you think like that?

Q: It's possible.

Q: No, no. If Master says that, that is what the Master says.

PR: All preceptors and no children makes the place dull. [laughter]

9

Wednesday, July 13, 1988

PR: My Master told me that, "There should be a training course. You will learn. I learned whatever I could." Perhaps that is why I am here. And he learned in the same way that I am trying to teach you. He made me do it. He did not teach me theory. He said, "I am going to give a sitting. You sit and watch and tell me what I am doing." If I was wrong, he said, "This is what you did, it should not be done that way." For instance, once I was giving a cleaning in Stella's house in Switzerland to that man I made a preceptor, who never came back. You remember? And in one cleaning Babuji was watching, and something I did, you know, in trying to clear the grossness, I sort of broke it up into pieces in my mind. He immediately stopped me. He said, "Do not do that." I said, "Do not do what? You told me to clean, I am cleaning." He said, "No, that is all right, but do not break it up into bits. Because if they break up too small, we cannot locate them, and they remain in the system, each one will become the focus of growth again." So, you want a Master like that, you see, to really teach you something. And I had him. So I learnt. Now I hope what I learnt I can teach you, and try to make you learn by doing in the same way, you see. Sit and do it.

Similarly, I told you, when we were first going to the States in 1972, sitting in the plane from London to New York, he said, "Prepare America." I said, "How to do it?" He said, "You know! Do not ask foolish questions." [laughter] And he lit his cigarette. And I closed my eyes and started working. After ten minutes, he said, "You are doing good work, but you know, this part of America, I do not know what is the name." In his mind he drew a map, he said, "Here, your transmission is not reaching." And it was correct. He could see it and I could see it too. Then I asked him, "If you know all this, why don't you do it yourself [he laughs] [laughter] and allow me to smoke?" He said, "Because when you do this, I can do some higher work."

So you see, preceptors assist in a very real way. The more they take over the work of the Master, the more the Master is relieved to take over yet higher work. Isn't it? And that is how growth comes. Such a man has to be promoted, you see. You want to wait until promotion to do the work. Here, you do the work, and even God cannot deny you that promotion. That was my experience in my company life, too. Even when I was the junior-most salesman, I was doing the work of my boss and inevitably, you know, I got his job. Do you know, in three years I was my boss's boss, in my company. So all comes by work. Work teaches, work gives, work elevates, work makes you grow. Work is its own reward. By doing work, you work more. The more you work, the more you work. The more you work, the more you get.

Q: Anyway, there is one thing that is sure, we cannot become your boss, if we work.

PR: You should try. [laughter] I would welcome anybody trying it. It is good, you see. Every father likes his son to come and tell him, "Dad, I can do better than that!" [laughter] Yes, when my son tells me, I am very happy. My father used to get angry. "No, no, you cannot talk to your father like that." I said, "Leave him alone," you know, it is like a tiger cub which tries to fight its old man, Hrroowwn [he growls]. The old tiger, it waits patiently, the father avoiding the cub, but when it gets a little too much, with one swipe of its paw it pushes it back. But that is how the child must develop — by trying to become the

Wednesday, July 13, 1988

father. Every child puts on his father's shoes, puts on his father's shirt and walks around pretending to be papa. Haven't you seen it? That through emulation only we can become, you see. We like to become that which we love. You allow the love to grow, the becoming will be automatic. You try to cut the becoming, the love goes. You see, all these things, they are simple homilies, you know, and we should know by experience. "Yes, my son, not only become like me, surpass me!" And then he says, "Come on, Dad, you don't really mean it." "Yes, of course, I mean it." Which father would like his son to be only like him? You see, suppose you are earning one hundred marks a month. Would you like your son only to earn one hundred marks a month? You would say, "Come on, Andreas, you can do better than that." "No, no, Dad, that is all you did." "Well, that should not be your limit, son. That is my destiny, my stupidity, my so many things, you see. But you are better stuff than that."

Now that is what we should do — how to make the son develop. Otherwise evolution would stop, if every son is a little less than his father. In thirty generations there would be no humanity left. But we are developing all the time. We can never be greater than the father, in the sense that a father is always a father, a son is always a son. My Master is always my Master. I am always his disciple. Isn't it? That situation can never change. But to say that I can never do the work that he did, I mean, it is a weakness. My Master would be the first man to be ashamed. "Is this all that I produced in you, you stupid fool?" I mean, he should think like that. Last question.

Q: You just now said, "Work, work, work!" But there is a limit to the worldly work, if it starts interfering with the spiritual growth.

Courmettes

PR: I do not know, I never had this problem. I mean, anybody who had known me from my early days with Babuji can tell you that I never had problems. I did my work, I did my company's work, I did my family work, all in the same spirit. All together, you see. I did not compartmentalize my life. When I went on tour, I also did my spiritual work.

Q: But then should one treat it as worship?

PR: Treat it as work. As work to be done. That is enough. I never worshiped my work. Sometimes, I despised it, but I still did it. Work is to be done. The weather is clearing up. [laughter] I have two more days to go. [laughter] The weekend — it can be what it likes.

Q: A real glint in your eyes right then. [laughter]

PR: Well, I heard all of it from my Master. [laughter] You see, that is how a teacher should be. Teach you to be happy, joyful **and** a good worker. Babuji was asked to eat chicken essence or something because he was very weak. Chicken essence, you know, it comes in ampoules. He asked Lalaji, "They say either eat chicken or take chicken essence. Should I do it?" Lalaji said, "Do not ask me this question, because if I tell you, 'You can,' all the other abhyasis will say, 'Aha, chicken is permitted.' [laughter] And they will start eating." So Babuji asked Lalaji, "What shall I do?" He said, "I have given you your work. Anything that is necessary to keep you healthy to do my work is permitted. You decide what is necessary." It is a very clear statement. Therefore he had his powers; for the moment, what he needed, it was given.

You never keep powers. Powers are for work. But we want power without working. What will you do with it if you are not working? It is like money when we do not want to spend it. What is the use of keeping it? The most essential thing is that, when I need it, I should have it. Thus, if you go in conformity

Wednesday, July 13, 1988

with the laws of nature, in obedience to your Master's work and principles, you get what you need. When you want to cut bread, you want a bread knife. Isn't it? You do not want a skiver. Sometimes I make that mistake. A knife looks very nice, you know, Wilkinson, big knife, beautiful stainless steel. I have got one at home which I have never used. [laughter]

Q: Was there any occasion where a preceptor, for example, being inquisitive, he decided to read the condition of Master?

PR: Well, it is a valuable exercise. I have tried it two or three times. And whenever I tried it, I went into samadhi. The first time I did it in Shahjahanpur, you know, we were sitting in Babuji's inside room. [he laughs] Most amusing. We were seventeen or eighteen of us and, you know, he used to sit facing the door and on this side under the switch near Lalaji's bed, there were some senior people. I think Justice Chaturvedi from Allahabad was there. I think it was before Basant. Half a dozen people were present. On this side were the youngsters like myself, the comparative juniors, you see. Babuji gave us a sitting. This strange idea came to me that during the sitting I will study Babuji's condition. [laughter] I do not know what happened, you know, and when it happened. Suddenly I found somebody [Chariji pats his own shoulder] you know, "Parthasarathi, Parthasarathi." And it was Babuji. There was nobody else left in the room. [laughter] I said, "Where are the others?" "Oh, they went out long ago," he said. [laughter] I said, "You mean you stopped the sitting and I am still here?" He said, "*Ha hun*, you know, I think you wanted to study something and..." [laughter] He knew it, you see. And he just locked me up. Nearly two hours I had been sitting there. [laughter] And he had to wake me up. Then he smiled very nicely, he said, "Knowledge is useful, but not always necessary." [laughter] That was one occasion when I tried it.

Courmettes

The second time I did it was when we were in Italy. He was extremely sick. He had been sick in Switzerland and Germany before that and we were going from I think Geneva to Rome. The direct flight was canceled. After two hours of hassling, running around, we got on a flight which was, I think, Geneva, Torino, Milano, Roma, you see. And it was something put together, you know, like an omelette for an unexpected guest. No water on the flight, no milk, no food, nothing. And Master was getting thirsty, he was feeling hot, and the one and a quarter hour flight took us nearly four hours. When we went to Rome, we were diverted away from one airport to the other, the older airport. And there was no customs, no immigration, everything was closed because we were unexpected. We had to wait two hours in the sun for the bus to come from the centre of the city. There was nobody to meet us. Eventually at 2:30 I landed up in the city with him. They dropped us in the centre of the city. I had no money. That was the day the pound had been floated, a historical day.

You see, everything was closed. No *cambio*, no exchange, nothing. I had not one lire, you see. So I left Babuji with the baggage on the pavement, and I said, "You stay here, for heaven's sake, do not move." I went around and eventually found a coffee shop. I said, "Can you exchange some money." He said, "I will give you only lower exchange. The standard rate I cannot give you." I said, "What is the right exchange?" "Some 1800 lire to the pound." "How much will you give me?" "1500." I said, "Done." So I changed ten pounds. He did not have more. And with that I took a taxi. And when I came out, which was after nearly half an hour's search for the exchange, Babuji was lying on the pavement. Can you imagine that? In Rome, on the pavement, a man like Babuji lying on the pavement with nothing under him? He was so sick. Then I had to lift him and put him in the taxi. Now, Saravanamuttu used to

Wednesday, July 13, 1988

live in Casal Palocco. I told the taxi driver to take us to Casal Palocco. Unfortunately within about three kilometres of Rome centre there is a hotel called Casal Paluta. He was going in the wrong direction, but I did not know any Italian and I said, "Not here, this way." He said something, and we ended up in the Hotel Casal Paluta. I said, "Not this," then I showed him the address. "Oh," he said, "Ostia." I said, "*Si*, Ostia." Then we went thirty-two kilometres to Ostia.

When we went there, there was nobody except a servant maid. I had to carry Babuji inside. And then all the people who had been in the other airport, they came back. By then they had known the flight was diverted. Babuji was totally unconscious, literally. On the bus, you know, he said something I have never heard him say. He said, "Today, I will not reach home alive." Can you imagine my condition? Then when these people came, we got the doctor. We had to move forty-eight hours later back to India. This was all after that three months trip, USA, Europe, everything, you see. The doctor said, "Stupid, he cannot be moved for a month. At least one month he has to stay here."

On that occasion, I again studied his condition, and did cleaning. And while I was doing it Toni came, you see, and Birthe. You remember I was doing cleaning for Babuji? And then Toni, she was fighting with me later. She said, "How can you clean the Master?" I said, "That is my business." It is like the doctor is sick and the junior says, "How can I treat my doctor, you see. He is my professor, he is the senior." He is sick. You have to do something, you know. And I did nearly forty minutes. I just sat, and I went into samadhi while I did the cleaning. He was better. Then, at that time he did not say anything. In the evening when he was able to sit up a little, he said, "You know that cleaning you did, it was very effective." [laughter] Even in his unconsciousness, he was conscious of who was doing what. That was the second time. The third time was in the hospital when he was dying.

So you see, it is possible, we can see more and more as he reveals. You can never learn unless he allows you to learn. This is the first fundamental of spiritual knowledge. No amount of *tapasya*, no amount of begging, no amount of anything else, you see, can give you that knowledge. Spiritual knowledge has to be revealed by the Master. You follow? And when he is willing to teach you, you must be open.

See, one day here I tried an experiment. I think it was the third week. I said, "Today all of you be especially receptive during the sitting." And it was a wonderful experience. I do not know if any of you were here that day. It was an absolutely fantastic experience. Because I had requested them in advance, they were prepared to co-operate and they felt the full thing. I did not do anything wonderful. But normally they sit at 7:00 for meditation, you know, with the thought of breakfast, "What it is this *baguette*," and you know, uncomfortable changing of cushions, pushing this way, mosquitoes. But when you tell them, "Please be extra alert today," they are willing to be alert.

So teaching means co-operation from the taught. That is real teaching. A good teacher elicits co-operation, he does not really teach. Then they teach themselves. So I am thankful to all of you for your co-operation. [laughter] And the measure of your learning will be reflected in the measure of your co-operation. When I say read, you must read. "No, no, what is it you are trying to do?" you know. Babuji never said, "Read." Why didn't he? It fails, because no one attempts it!

Q: In your very young days you must have been a naughty boy. [laughter]

PR: Shall I tell you a secret? My Master loved it. [laughter] Because everybody was trying to be so sober and so saintly in

Wednesday, July 13, 1988

his presence, you know, hypocrites. I was myself. And he loved me to be myself, and for me to treat him as himself. I did not make a God out of my Master, you see. He was my God. But to me he was also very human. I used to joke with him, I used to push him like this sometimes and the other people, well, you know, were angry. "Oh, no, you cannot touch Master." I asked, "Why not?" Then I think it was this old man Ishwar Sahai, he said, "Do you know, if you touch him you can get a shock." [laughter] I said, "For you perhaps but not for me."

And when we were in Europe, every day I had to bathe him, towel him. You know I had to, especially in Gangloff's house, there was no tap. The only water source was in the bathtub itself. So I had to draw the curtain, open the taps, adjust the water to his temperature, then lift him inside, draw the curtain, take out his *dhoti* from inside, you know. He was very shy! You know that. Take out his *banian* and what-not one by one, close it properly, see that he is bathed, then pass him the towel. And he would come out dripping like a child. Because he would only know to put the towel around himself like that. Then I had to towel him. While toweling him I would just give him a hug, you know, a squeeze. And he used to love it. "Humm, Humm, Humm, Humm," [he imitates Babuji chuckling] [laughter]

You see, that man was starving for some human love and affection. Everybody put him on a pedestal, and gave him *prasad*. "Babuji, why don't you heal my sick child, why don't you see my this, why don't you make my wife co-operate with me?" What is all this? He was, he **is** God. But he was also a human being, you see. And he wanted us to love him as a human being, worship him as a God, follow him as a Master. You know, we have to learn to see him in all these things. That is why I gave those two talks, *Balanced Existence*. Read it. Either we make the mistake of treating him only as human, or

Courmettes

only as Divine. And we lose the benefit of his association. If he is only God, you might as well go to the temple and worship some God there. And if he is only a human being, well, you have your father and mother and your wife at home. It is precisely because he is everything in between. That treatment only I gave him, you know. Nobody else had the courage; and not the perception, I should say. Even when he was sick, people used to say, "Oh, this is a divine drama. How can Master be sick?" What do you mean how can Master be sick? And they used to leave him there and sit down and make merry, like we are doing here, you know.

So we have to see the human in the divine, and the divine in the human, in one thing, you see. Matter in spirit and spirit in matter. Then we learn to accept that everything can be in one. All in one. Not just three in one, oil for the Singer sewing machine! All in one. And that is the beauty of this ultimacy, you know. How can God be only God? You tell me. He has to be everything in his creation. So, he must be a man, he must be a human. He must have the foibles of humanity, the penchant for an occasional joke, the seriousness, a certain sudden burst of temper, when it is necessary, certain tastes in food. He liked the chapati and dahl, mushroom soup when he came to Europe, everybody knows. "Why should Babuji like mushroom soup?" People have asked, you see. "Oh, it means the Master has taste." Yes, why not? I expect my Master to have taste, in music, in food. Isn't it? I would not like to be a disciple of a Master who had no taste. My Master was absolutely a man of taste. He dressed well. He liked clean clothes. He liked to look happy and charming.

And when he was happy he used to sit regally like that, you know, there is a photograph. [laughter] I mean, he looks more an emperor, like any emperor looks. [laughter] And that is the real grace of the Master. When he was sick, he looked

Wednesday, July 13, 1988

sick. He did not try to bluff. When he was in pain he said, "I am having pain." When the doctor came with the injection needle, he would wince. [laughter] Some people may think, "What is this divinity which is afraid of an injection needle?" I used to tell them, "I will bring a knife, you wait, let me see your divinity." [laughter] Of course! I used to be very annoyed with some of our seniors, "No, no, no, you see, this is not correct. He must give a good example, you see. A saint must bear pain." I said, "Who said so?" Here is a question of sensitivity. He must feel even the tiniest pain. How can he respond to your pain unless he feels his pain himself, isn't it? Therefore, he was the perfect Master. He felt everything that we felt, and he could respond. If you are like a man of stone, you know, "No, no, there is no pain, there is no heartache, there is no this, there is no that." You are a stone. *N'est-ce pas*? (Isn't it?)

Q: But we have to develop sensitivity.

PR: Who?

Q: We all.

PR: Yes, of course. Therefore, you know, we are sensitive to pleasures. But when we become sensitive to pain, we start, you know, "Kicking against the traces," as they say in English. We do not want to feel it. It is like a camera which will take only white objects and not black objects. Is it possible? If the film is sensitive it has to take everything. So we have to learn to be sensitive and not feel the pain. Feel the pain, but not be affected by it. Therefore constant remembrance helps. Yes, okay, this is what you are suffering from — clean! Now that pain goes, your pain also goes.

Preceptors are agitated that they do not read now. They will read, because it is the process which is being taught, not the result which is being shown. It is like teaching someone to cook. The first time it may be a failure. You burn the eggs, or even the toast. Every new bride burns the toast. She cannot stop cooking.

Q: I do.

PR: You still do?

Q: I still do. But the toaster's not working right.

PR: So you are an ever new bride. [laughter]

So you see, it is the process we have to learn. The result will come when the process is mastered. Now we want immediate results, you know. The first time you are taught something, you want the result. Well, some are lucky, they get the result. Some have to work a little more. But they know now what to expect, what to do. It is like anything, where you cannot show the result. It is like telling a man who has never seen a boulder, "When you go on the road, if there is a boulder, stop, remove it and then walk on." And he walks on, and every small pebble he finds he thinks is a boulder, and removes it!

There is a famous story, you know, about a man, a gullible fellow, who was in the south of India, in a district where there is no river, no water, a sort of parched land. But he had this craving for spirituality. So he went to a Master. The Master said, "Go north and you will find a big river, it is called the Ganges. Those who bathe in it will get salvation." He walked twenty, thirty miles and it was long enough for him, for a villager who has never left his village. There he saw one ditch full of water, you see, waste water. He said, "Oh, Guruji said a big body of water. This must be it." He pitched his tent and was there ten years bathing in that dirty water.

And after ten years, one day, a guru came. He said, "What are you doing here? This is, you know, a ditch." He said, "No, my Master said bathe in the big river that will come to you in

Wednesday, July 13, 1988

the north called the Ganges, and I have traveled so much north, you know, this is the first big thing." He said, "No, no, it is much bigger, you walk ahead." So he went on, then he came to a small irrigation channel. He said, "This is it, you see, what a foolishness I made." He sat there and ten years he was bathing there. Then a guru came. He said, "What are you doing, this is an irrigation channel. That river is still north." He said, "Oh, I am grateful to you, you see, you are putting me on the right path." Then he walked on. Came to one of the rivers of India, which is yet not the holy river. Like this he went on, but he never reached the Ganges. He died.

The other masters who guided him also died. Judgement! this man was sent to Heaven; the gurus were sent to Hell. [laughter] And they protested to God, you see, "What is this?" God said, "He, in his innocence, thought every river was the Ganges and he was benefiting by his faith. What do you think is in the river? There is nothing in the river, you see, it is the faith that makes you change! You people had no faith. On the contrary you destroyed his faith, therefore you go to Hell. You, as a master, should have had the ability to strengthen his faith. Instead of that, you destroyed it. Therefore I am sending you to a place of correction. I hope you will learn to have faith, that Ganges is where I say it is, not where the river flows!" [he laughs] This lesson we have to learn, you know.

So it is necessary to learn the process. Like in a chemical laboratory, you know, in school, they teach you how to handle a pipette, a burette, conical flasks, round-bottomed flasks, weighing balances. You know initially it is tricky to weigh to one hundredth of a gram or one thousandth of a gram. Even to move this, you know, so that the pan remains balanced, it takes a little time. To focus a microscope on a specimen slide without breaking the slide, it takes time. Some people get the knack, while other fellows like me, you know, the first time I smashed the slide, and I had to pay twenty-five rupees, apart from a lashing from my teacher. He said, "You do not know even how to do this!" What to do? You learn slowly, you see. Because it is layer after layer, and the thing you want to see may be in one of these layers. You focus on the top layer. You do not see anything, and the other things are hazy, then you focus on the next. Like when you have a photograph, you see, sometimes the foreground is fuzzy, the man in the back is in focus. Depends on what you want.

Q: Chari. May I ask a question? Can one fall back from a given point?

PR: It is possible. Yes.

Q: You can fall back?

PR: Yes, yes. It is possible. If you are not doing the thing. Well, at least static is very easy. Like a car, you know. If you take your foot off the accelerator, inevitably it slows. Because friction is there. In a frictionless surface you maintain motion. But where there is friction involved, you inevitably slow. That is why you remove your foot from the accelerator before you press the brake. That is additional braking. Otherwise the road friction will itself take care of stopping you.

Q: So one can fall back?

PR: Yes, but you know that it is possible, so why are you worried about it? That something is possible, should not worry us. You know, it is possible that I die. Why possible? It is sure, isn't it?

Q: I mean, I nearly always have the feeling that I cannot keep the condition which I have when I am in your presence.

PR: Yes. But that is because, you see, there are two reasons. One: it is true in the sense that you are now feeling the absence, whereas you should feel the presence.

Wednesday, July 13, 1988

Q: So it does not mean that one really has gone back.

PR: It does not mean anything like that. It is like, you know, you think somebody is with you in the room, and you are doing your work, and suddenly you look around and you do not find the person there, and you feel afraid. You know, children have this. The mother is sitting and the child is studying. Quietly the mother moves away to her kitchen, or somewhere else. The child looks around, there is nobody, it is terrified. Now who created this condition? It created it for itself. We are supposed to feel the presence, not when the person is present. Then what is there to feel? He is **there**.

Q: But it can also be the contrary. You think you do not feel very much in the presence, and you feel more when you are absent.

PR: Actually the presence should be felt when he is not there. Isn't it? When he is there, you do not have to feel the presence you see the person. No? What is there to feel? Of course if he is naughty and giving you trouble you will feel something else, you see. [laughter] Or if he is rude and calling you names, you will feel something else. But the person himself, or herself, you do not have to feel. You remember, so many times I told you, after Babuji passed away, people feel his presence more strongly. Why? Because when he was alive, we located him in Shahjahanpur. "Babuji is in Shahjahanpur." Automatically you remove him from your presence. Now you feel his presence because He was always everywhere. Now he is everywhere because the body does not interfere with your feeling. His body.

Q: I did not think of points until I came here.

Q: Are you using condition and approach interchangeably?

PR: They are two different things.

Q: We say God has no mind; now when your Master has passed away, does he keep his mind?

PR: Yes. He must! If he has merged, then he has no individual mind.

Q: Yes. But how can he really be in contact, or like Lalaji being in contact?

PR: Lalaji retained his existence. He made a promise to his disciple that, "Until your work is done and you come back to me, I shall not leave for the other world."

Q: Well, this is naturally a very difficult question, in my mind, and somebody being close to him, we can still retain the mental contact?

PR: No, but it does not matter, you see. God has no mind. Matter is inert. But if you create a vacuum, you can draw matter into yourself. I do not see why, if your vacuumization is perfect, you cannot draw wisdom down, from wherever it is, even from God. He may not be able to act, but you can act. That is why the human being is always the agency of divinity on earth. God cannot work directly on earth. Therefore saints or great people come, one after the other, you know, age after age. Precisely because they have the mind, they have the heart. They can assess, they can feel, and they can respond. That is why in Sanskrit, we say, "*daivam maanusha rupena.*" (God comes in the form of a human being). So, it is very simple.

Q: Now that Babuji has left this world, is he still able to exert an effect?

PR: It depends, you know, whether he thinks it should be done. Like Lalaji did occasionally. You have read in *My Master*, that he has given me sittings when he thought my Master was not able to do so, or was not able to think of the right way of doing it. He comes to help him. Not for us. That he gave me the sitting

Wednesday, July 13, 1988

is of no special merit, as far as I am concerned. It was to help his disciple that he came. "You are having difficulty with this fellow. Send him to me." It is like you are a doctor, and you tell your assistant, "Are you having any trouble with that guy? If so, you send him to me." Isn't it? You are not directly interested in the guy who comes to you, but in your assistant, and in his performance for that person. So unless there is a need, they will not interfere. They can, but they will not. Why on earth should they? When you send your assistants to various wards, you do not follow them around and see what they are doing. Initially perhaps, while they are in training, later on, not at all. And I do not think it is any merit of the disciple if his Master has to interfere at every stage and give instructions and this and that. It also proves the failure of the Master himself. That his training was inadequate. Minimum interference. Only when necessary. That is the proof of the assistant's ability.

Q: May I ask one question? If an abhyasi sees Babuji in sittings, is it actually your mind that contacts him?

PR: Maybe, or maybe a direct perception. Why should we have the doubt? I see Babuji. I do not ask, "Where do I see him, in Shahjahanpur or here?" I am happy to see my Master. Suppose I see him in a vision a thousand miles away. It is no use. When I see him, I want him here. No?

Q: Is it possible to have a reading of your own condition?

PR: Yes, tomorrow's exercise. [laughter] It is possible. It is like an author asking, "Can I read my own book?" Why not?

Q: Sister Kasturi told me one time that we could not read other people's conditions until we could read our own.

PR: It is not correct.

Q: But, I mean, even if you read your own book, it is very difficult to say whether it is good or bad.

PR: That is all right. But you can read. No? That is what I said. Reading is something, judgement is something else.

Q: Yes. That is true.

PR: You see, you give me, say, Einstein's book on general relativity. I can read it. But I may not make head or tail of it. Because I know the language, I read it. But understanding is something else. Then acting on that understanding to apply his equations, promote it further, I have to be, you know, a genius. Isn't it? It is said that in all this world, there are only about eight people who really know what Einstein said. Eight! And everybody is talking of Einstein all the time; books are written about him. And this is a statement made by one of the great minds of science, you know, not by any flippant chemist or physicist. He said, "There are possibly eight people in this whole world who understand Einstein and his physics." It is like saying, "I understand my Master's work, only when I become like him."

See, like a child is always critical of its parents. When it becomes the mother or the father, then it understands why they behaved like that. "Yes, now I understand, you know, my old man. I was always quarreling with that fellow. Now I understand why he was like that. My kids, you know, they have taught me so many things." So the kids teach you why your father behaved in such a way. You see how knowledge comes. But you have to have the kid first. No?

So that is why we can understand something only when we are in that situation ourselves. Somebody falls into a ditch, it may be only two metres deep, it is night, he thinks he has fallen down a deep gorge and he is shouting. Then along comes a good samaritan with his flashlight, and he says, "Why are you bawling? It is only two metres." He says, "Yes, for you, but for me [he laughs] it is something else."

Wednesday, July 13, 1988

So there is the objective and there is the subjective. So, many problems, and the first lesson to learn in all this spiritual work is that you must erase yourself. Suppose a mirror forms opinions about the faces it reflects and says, "No, no. I do not like this face which I see before me. Let me modify it a little and show it to you." You will never see your face. Isn't it? So we have got to be objective. No self is involved there. That is why Babuji used to say, "Make your mind utterly blank. You will see everything in this universe." Why only man or child or woman or dog? You will see everything in the universe. You look at the tree, you see its essence.

Q: Can the preceptor do something wrong? Or is it not possible?

PR: Not possible.

Q: The abhyasi is always protected.

PR: Yes. The system is like that. It is not protection or anything. The system is fail-safe.

Q: Unless a preceptor talks too much.

PR: Even then you cannot do harm.

Q: Okay, I continue. [laughter]

Q: And when an abhyasi is practising since many years and only has very slow progress, is it for sure his own fault, or can the preceptor have a part in it?

PR: It can be even Master's fault. I mean, to be charitable to the abhyasi. [laughter] Why not? I know many instances where Babuji said, "You know, this thing, it is my fault, because something I should have done, I did not do." What is a fault? I mean, there is nothing to be ashamed of in a fault. You go to sleep at night, you do not switch off your transistor, next morning the battery is drained. Is it a crime? "Oh," you say, "I am sorry, I forgot to switch it off." Of course, if your husband is nasty, he can say, "You stupid fool, you are always doing this." But, it still does not make it a crime. Mistakes occur. They are to be rectified. So what is wonderful about making a mistake? Without making a mistake, you never learn. Isn't it? I would like to go on making mistakes. Only thing is, I do not want to make the same mistake a second time.

Q: Forgetfulness, Chariji. Sometimes it happens that you mention a certain thing that you forgot that you had mentioned. And then your friend comes along and says, "You mentioned this to me." You ask, "I mentioned it to you?" You may have said something perhaps a day earlier, or a few hours earlier, but you cannot remember it.

PR: Well, it is a good sign. Spiritually speaking, it is good. But do not forget in which bank you have your accounts. [laughter]

Q: I always thought you had a good memory.

PR: Who?

Q: You.

PR: He is not talking about me. [laughter] He is talking about himself. My memory is not really a memory. Think over it. [laughter]

Q: Like a tape recorder?

PR: No, no.

Q: It is the *akashic* records. [laughter]

PR: Well, think over it. Then you will, perhaps, learn how to develop it, too.

Q: Chari, the content of the lecture you gave yesterday seemed to me something that could be shared. Is it going to be available for all abhyasis?

PR: Abhaysis? I do not know. I will have to see what I said first.

Wednesday, July 13, 1988

Q: Because it seems like it contains so many things which are so sensible and should be widely known.

PR: I have to either listen to the tapes or read the transcripts and then decide. Because, you know, it is like a train which moves — it moves. Having moved on, what it has moved over is forgotten. Otherwise it would never get where it has to go to. Isn't it? So, I go like that. I speak and I do not know what I have spoken, except that I have a feeling that it was right or not right. And that feeling comes, perhaps, out of some inner justification. Not necessarily a judgement of what I did, or said, but something in me which says, "Yes, it is okay." Not to every detail, not to this, that, or the other, but in sum and substance, it was okay.

Q: In any case, this is a major opening altogether, what you do here. This is something completely new.

PR: Well, I have been wanting to do this for many years. Right from 1967 when I was made a preceptor. I have been suggesting it to Babuji, and Babuji agreed it should be done. But he was always reluctant to go against the wishes of the senior preceptors. He did not want to create problems. And he said, "If I tell them, they would not understand. If I ask them to do, they will not do. So I let them learn in their own way." I said, "But they are not learning." He said, "No man can learn unless he knows that he does not know."

10

Thursday, July 14, 1988

Q: In the last days, I have felt rather exhausted sometimes. Is it just physical or spiritual?

PR: It is the imbalance between your spiritual self and your physical self. It is like a material which breaks down under pressure. Wax melts under heat, but wax can be made not to melt by mixing it with certain other things. Isn't it? Like you have alloys. So here we are being alloyed in a different way, you see. The Master, by putting himself in you, through his transmission, is changing you. As Babuji said, every atom in the body is changed, but until the process is complete, you have always the problem of accepting. Not accepting with the mind, but the body accepting, you see. Now, if the mind is strong the body co-operates, like you have these famous instances of the crucifixion and all, somebody being burnt at the stake. They do not react, because the mind has such a supreme control over the body, you see. The pain becomes something irrelevant — virtually not there. But until then if the mind is also weak, or not strong enough, let us say, not weak, and the body is unable to accept that sort of higher vibration in it, it gives us this sort of temporary fatigue, tiredness. Sometimes even emotional stress is caused. For no reason at all, you sit down and weep. You do not know why. It is a mixture of suffering due to inability to bear, and the longing for that which you are unable to bear. It is a very odd sort of mixture.

Q: And if the body is feeble, if the weakness is in the body?

PR: It is the same thing.

Q: Is it not the effect of cleaning?

PR: Cleaning will always improve, unless you drop the object, [he chuckles] suppose you are washing a glass. [laughter] But, of course, here, because it is a human system, I gave you that example, you know, cleaning can never cause harm. So, it is for your good. And all the lightness that you feel during a sitting is not due to transmission at all, it is due to cleaning. Cleaning gives you lightness. Transmission, when you are light, gives you the feeling of going deep into the meditation. Transmission, when it is gross, produces vibrations, all these funny things, you see. The subtler it is, the more you must feel that there has been nothing happening in the meditation. But after the sitting is over you feel the difference. These are some things we should know, you see.

Q: Even if you have thoughts?

PR: Thoughts are not important. It is whether you attend to them or not that is important.

Q: So in the physical plane, it is within that plane, it can give stress to that organ only?

PR: Which?

Q: Transmission.

PR: Transmission cannot give stress. You see, when the system is clean, you have a state of thoughtlessness, or of near thoughtlessness. Thoughtlessness is not a spiritual condition, it is a condition where your inside is evacuated of all grossness, almost all grossness, so that there is no thought to come up from inside, you see. Now you can receive thoughts from outside, you are pure now. It can be divine thought, it can be Master's instructions. They come from outside. Now they are no longer your thoughts. They cannot disturb you. In that condition, when you receive a transmission, you are able to plunge — straight, you see. Otherwise, it is like a man wearing his boots, his

Thursday, July 14, 1988

military uniform, his hat, goggles and trying to dive into the pool.

Q: So, this inner silence comes from the vacuum.

PR: Yes. *Exactement!* (Exactly)

Q: And when we give a sitting to an abhyasi, and we feel very strong vibrations, what does that mean?

PR: Normally you should not feel vibration when you give a sitting. Maybe, instead of giving a sitting she is taking a sitting herself. It is possible, without being conscious, you know, that you get into meditation yourself. Open your eyes and start again.

Q: Chari, last night you were saying that this system is completely failsafe and the preceptor could never do any harm. In your talk this morning, you told us about instances where preceptors have done harm and can do harm.

PR: Only preceptors in the central region.

Q: Oh! It is a very unusual case.

PR: Very unusual case. You see, Babuji has told me that there have been several occasions when he has been a little inattentive and some harm has happened. See, suppose I trust you and I give you a job. I do not supervise you thinking, "Well, Fred is an elevated boy and he is capable." At that moment, if you become egotistic and try to show what you can do, there is this sort of damage possible. And also when a man in the central region works, the power is there, you see. Otherwise, you have to check in such a way, that he cannot work at all. That is not possible. So, it is only by, it is a surprising thing, that damage is possibly only by the elevated preceptors, you see. And that, you see, in the Mission today, what is happening, it is happening only from the elevated levels. I mean, that is always the case. A brick, when it falls from here (a large height) only kills.

Isn't it? If it is on the floor, at the most, you may stub your toe on it. So elevation carries with it the potential for both. Therefore cleaning is more and more important. As Babuji said, "Do not give power without cleaning." That is why these three preparatory sittings, which can be, or which generally are, even more sometimes. Babuji said once he gave twenty-two sittings to a man before starting transmission. Then, this danger is reduced.

Q: You said that so far nobody is in the central region in the West. Do you think it will be possible in the future, with your help?

PR: With your co-operation. [laughter] Well, Babuji wants, you know, everywhere. It is not reserved for the one or the other. It is reserved only for the deserving. Be deserving, and you get. Very simple. Be deserving! All things are possible with love and devotion. With practise, if you depend on practise alone, it may not be possible. Because in spirituality, the highest law, Babuji has said so many times, you must have heard him saying it, "Only he gets, to whom He desires to give." That is why all this is a preparation to attract his attention towards us.

Q: At what time the practice can stop? At what level, I mean?

PR: Oh! When your inner state is almost always in a state of constant remembrance, contemplation. Then what is the need of meditation? One day I had these Danish children in my room, you know, about fifteen or sixteen of them. Two hours, three hours, they were with me with all sorts of questions. One child asked me a question, "Do you meditate for yourself?" [laughter] I said, "No, I do not meditate." "No, no, but then why don't you meditate? Because Babuji has said it is necessary." [laughter] I said, "Yes, but I have so much work to do: I have no time." Then that child said, "That is no excuse." [uproarious laughter]

Thursday, July 14, 1988

And then, finally I had to say, Babuji himself told me, "You need not meditate now, provided you give that time to my work." And then she asked me, "When can I stop meditation? When I start it, you know, when can I stop it?" [laughter] I said, "Under the same condition. That you have so much work to do that your Master says, 'Stop meditation and give that time to the work', then you can also stop." Then they all looked at each other very solemnly, you know, and said, "We have to work." [laughter] [he laughs] It was really nice. They asked all sorts of questions including, I believe, one question, whether I have already selected the next representative or not. [laughter] You see, they are concerned so much with Sahaj Marg, while only children. If this is to be fostered and made to develop, it is the parents' responsibility, you see. Because it is there already, the seed is there. You can see the seedling coming up.

Q: How old were these children?

PR: Oh, between the age of six and eleven or twelve.

Q: Some are already fourteen.

PR: Only Kasturi, you see, not the others. All the others are below ten, most of them. Kasturi is only thirteen, not fourteen.

Q: Actually, Kamela is fourteen.

PR: Kamela? So you see, they take so much interest. And they wanted to see me alone. They said, "No grown-ups." [he laughs] [laughter] You know, they wanted to go on a picnic. I promised that we will arrange it. We arranged the picnic. Then I had the deputation of the children here. "Chari, we do not want grown-ups." I said, "Why not?" "No, no, you know, we want to be only the kids." I said, "What about me? I am a grownup." "No, no, we are coming only with you." And then, one little one started saying, "You know, but if Chari comes, the whole Mission will be there with him." [laughter] [he laughs] So I said, "What shall we do?" So they were confused, you know:

without him, no picnic; with him, the whole Mission. [he laughs] [laughter] "What shall we do?" So I said, "You all go, and we will sit somewhere, and I will come and join you." They said not to go. You know, they were all here all over the place. We had picnic lunch from here and sat here eating it. And everybody enjoyed it. We will surely have many preceptors from these children, you know, in future. Do you want a sitting or not today? [laughter]

Q: Is it necessary?

PR: I thought of skipping it.

Q: We can have it later.

PR: At nine o'clock.

Q: Yes, nine o'clock.

PR: Okay, nine o'clock.

Q: What is the right age for children to start to say the prayer?

PR: Any age. Three years, when they start talking.

Q: And the meditation?

PR: Eighteen. In the case of exceptional children, even sixteen.

Q: You gave a sitting to my wife, she was two months pregnant. Does that have anything to do with it?

PR: It helps the child. Because it gets from the mother, not directly by itself. But once the child is born, then it becomes separated. You are now transmitting to the child. Here you are transmitting to the mother.

Q: Can you heal a child when he had a shock or something like this?

PR: You should not do anything.

Q: They see and try, for example, the parents are in meditation, and they sit and imitate. Is that okay?

Thursday, July 14, 1988

PR: Let them imitate. I have seen children, you saw in Khichcha, half a dozen children sitting in front of half a dozen children, each transmitting to the other according to them, you see. [laughter] This line is sitting giving sitting to that line. Five children here, five children there. But the most amusing was in Canada. You know, suddenly I went into a room, and there was Christine's daughter, Robyn, aged five, with a neighbor's child aged four and a half, or four. They were quarreling. The little fellow was telling Robin, "You know, I want to give you a sitting." "No, no," the elder one says, "No, no. I am Parthasarathi, you know. You sit, and I am Parthasarathi, I will give you a sitting." [laughter] And the other one was saying, "Why should you be Parthasarathi all the time? Now I want to be Parthasarathi?" [laughter] [he laughs] Five year old child! [he chuckles]

Q: It will make a nice article for the *Sahaj Shishu*.

PR: Yes, we have photographs of the children.

Q: Is it possible to visualize our children going towards the Master?

PR: You should not do anything. You see, the parents cannot do anything directly, but indirectly they can do everything. First, by becoming examples for the children to follow, you see. This is most important. And if we live the life in the right way the children automatically lead the life, in the right way. That is the importance of parenthood. That we provide the right environment, the right example. That is why I have always said that it is a big and onerous thing, you know, being a parent. Whether you are the father or mother is not relevant. We have to be alert. What is the use of a father, you know, smoking hash and telling his child, "You should not do it." And then when he starts doing it, the father cannot even muster the courage to tell him, "Do not do it," because he is guilty. I have known many families with this problem. I have known families where the son says, "Oh, come on Dad, you are doing it. Why don't you stop first?" That is why in the Hindu tradition, parentage, you know, is associated with systematic renunciation of so many things, one by one, one by one, until you finally renounce the family itself and walk off.

Q: How to handle resistance in your child at home?

PR: Resistance?

Q: Resistance to meditation and all these things? And he is involved in a Christian education.

PR: Well, without forcing, you know, you should show what is right, rather than tell what is right. It is always easy to preach, and to be dogmatic, and to insist. By your living you should show your children what is this, what is that. That is why it is said there are two ways of bringing up children: by example and by precept. We always try the precept, because to be an example is difficult. With the transmission, you know, we add suggestion, very light, very subtle.

Q: That is general, which does not go against one's attitude, I mean, it should be something in general, not to impose something, even if it is right.

PR: Well, if you look at that, everything is an imposition. When a man is drugging himself to death, and you tell him, "Do not do it," is it not an imposition? Why should he listen to you? Why should you tell him? See, on one side you talk of compassion and sympathy and help. How can you do it without imposition? A man is drowning in the river, it can be construed as an imposition if you pull him out. [he chuckles] Let us say he wants to commit suicide. Are you right in pulling him out of the river? Is it not an imposition that he wants to die and you want him to live? So, that is all, you know, not relevant. What is good for a person...

Thursday, July 14, 1988

Q: What we think is good, we do it.

PR: Well, at that moment, yes. If a man is sick you give him medicine. "Oh, no, but I do not want to impose, Chari. Unless he is able to ask." And if he is unconscious, who is he going to ask? Then you open his mouth and pour it in. It is even worse; it is physical imposition. You know, this is my opinion, that many couples have problems because of this. You know the husband comes for Sahaj Marg, he does not bring his wife in the beginning. He says, "I should not impose. She should come." After some time she refuses to come. She says, "You were never interested in me. Why didn't you take me? What is good for you, is it not good for me?" Then you cannot say, "No, no, you know, I did not want to impose." Are you not imposing everything else? How will you answer that wife? So, the right time is the beginning. And if you had done that and said, "Come, let us go," like we are going anywhere else, there also we go, there is no problem. But if you let it lie, after six months, eight months, one year, you cannot make her come at all. Then she starts rebelling against Sahaj Marg. "Now, why are you going there, leaving me alone?" Another problem now, you see. The problem has changed its aspect.

Q: Before introducing an abhyasi, often I ask to have a talk before to see, to adjust each other, and when it is a man I always ask...

PR: All that is unnecessary. You leave it to them, you see. I always suggest, when single people come, I say, "What about your wife?"

Q: Yes. That is what I...

PR: Then he says, "No, no, I will bring her next time," and they are there, you see. You do not suggest you have a talk together, and see it. Why? Why do you suggest? That becomes a suggestion, you see.

Courmettes

Q: Agreed.

PR: As if there is something wrong, and they should discuss and then come. Suppose you go to a sweet shop and you want to buy something. And he says, "You know, it is better you taste it first and then buy it." [he laughs] You would say, "Okay, give me something else." If the shopkeeper himself is in doubt, [he laughs] [laughter] who will buy?

Q: Their son does not want to follow his parents.

PR: Yes, at that stage, I told you it is too late, you know. When he was young and you had the chance, you should have introduced him to prayer; proved to him the merit of Sahaj Marg by his saying, "Oh, look how my papa has changed. What is this Sahaj Marg that has made him so human?" They must want to come, and you must tell them, "Sorry, you have to wait." You know how many children come to me, wherever I go? "No, no, I want to start meditation." I tell them, "Please wait." You have seen. Everywhere in India we go, there are children pestering me, you know. They write letters to me, children of thirteen and twelve. "Why I should not meditate? You see, if it is good for you, why is it not good for me?" Then I have to tell them, "It is very good, but not yet." I had to allow a girl of fifteen to start meditation. You know that? In Delhi.

Q: Yes.

PR: I had made a promise, you know, without thinking. I said, "Next October, or next September, you can begin." I forgot her age, or had miscalculated it. She was there on that date, and she was sitting, sitting, sitting, you know, looking at me very expectantly, and I did not know what she was looking expectantly for. Then I said, "What are you doing here? Shouldn't you be going to school?" She said, "Oh, you have forgotten." I said, "What?" "Remember the promise you made last year?" I said, "What?" Then she said, "You are supposed to give me

Thursday, July 14, 1988

a sitting today." I said, "But you are only fifteen." She said, "But you promised." [laughter] [he laughs] I had to give her a sitting.

Q: Generally the age was eighteen. Then Babuji said, "But if a child is very precocious even if they are five years old and insist on starting, you can you start them." I was astonished.

PR: The Master can decide. Certainly not five. You see, the only danger is that such a child, its tendencies will be turned totally towards spirituality, and it will be useless for this world. There is no other danger. So Sahaj Marg, you know, the two wings of the bird. Life has to be balanced. You cannot be totally in spirituality forgetting the world and lying like a vegetable. Therefore, the age of eighteen, you see. When the child knows what it wants, why it wants it, then it is right.

Yatra is something else, you see. Very much like cooking, you know. You read a cookery book, and it says, "Prepare the following: half a pound of flour, two eggs, one ounce of white sugar, one slip of parsley. Lay this aside." Very erudite, you know. Then he says, "Take the flour, put a pinch of salt and mix it with water, and knead thoroughly, set it aside, cover it with a wet cloth." Now, what do we do? "Mix the rest." [laughter] Then comes the grand conclusion. Which should I put first now? Cookery books never tell you. And that is why, when you have many things, we can easily confuse one for the other. Like every new bride sometimes puts salt instead of sugar in the coffee, and sugar instead of salt in the soup, because they look alike. So, here also, cleaning is something, tendency is something. Though tendencies come from samskara, the samskara is something else. Thoughts can be from within, or from without. "It is my thought," we say, but whose thought? That is why, when you are a saint, and the thought comes from above, you do not say, "It is my thought." And we also use it in colloquial language. "I had a thought." You do not say, "I think." Only in French you say, "*Je pense.*" [laughter] "I had a thought." "A thought came to me."

Q: What a disturbing thought that comes from outside?

PR: It can disturb. I mean, if it is of that nature. When you are sensitive, there is no filter. What comes, comes.

Q: How can you distinguish if it is from outside?

PR: It does not matter. Do not attend! If a fly is inside the room, does it come from inside or does it come from outside the room? [he chuckles] Will you ask the fly, [he laughs] "Are you from inside or the outside?" [laughter] But at the higher stages, when they come from Divinity, then you have to attend, you see, because generally it is an information you need, or an order which you have to execute.

Q: You quote Babuji very much and it is word for word, do you transfer yourself in that time?

PR: Yes, yes, I get most of my stuff like that. For instance, I quote Babuji so much, I put myself in that situation with him, and I speak. And it is all exactly what he said before. I cannot possibly remember all these things.

Q: Yes, but for people who did not know you, do you put yourself in a time frame by concrete memory of that time or just by thinking of that time?

PR: Just, I am there at that time. It is enough. How will you feel the environment in a particular time? You cannot define it, and then you do not feel it. You are projecting it. Say, I am in the year 1616, autumn, in Germany: what is the condition like? I must be able to feel it. That is how Babuji gave the experience of the condition when man was created for the first time, or human beings came into being. I have written, I think, somewhere.

Thursday, July 14, 1988

Q: And how was it?

PR: By putting himself in that situation and transmitting.

Q: And he got it, what was that condition?

PR: That you should find out. It is like saying, "You ate chocolate ice cream and pistachio ice cream. What was it like?" I say, "You eat and find out." We can transmit knowledge but not experience.

Q: I ask only because some people say, "When man was created it was by God." It is said, "In the image of God." Therefore...

PR: No, no. We are not talking of that creation. Here, on the planet earth. At that time everything was divine. Why only the human being? Even now all that God creates is divine, but we make of it profane.

Q: So therefore it can do harm. It can harm you to be a writer. If you have to put your feelings into a person and find out how it is, then you can be harmed?

PR: No, if you are separate from it nothing can harm you.

Q: But if you feel it?

PR: See, when you are a clinical person and you work with poisons in the laboratory, you wear gloves, put on a mask and you work. It does not harm you. But without the protection, if you do it, it is possible to be harmed. So we have the protection, which is to surround ourselves with the Master and have Him inside, all the time. Then nothing can come in. So the techniques are there, you see. We do not employ them.

PR: (about preceptors reading ability) As all these Western people say, "Put their nose to the grinding wheel." Except for two people who are wrong, most of them are right. And why they could not have done it all these years? Basically they need a stick.

Q: That is what I said, the first time I saw you with your stick.

PR: [he laughs] He is egging me on the path of disaster. [laughter] All that you need is to be encouraged to do it. *Mon Maitre a dit une fois: c'est necessaire.* (My Master said once, "It is necessary.")

Q: I have the feeling that they are talking about the reading of condition, but I have a feeling it is more the knowledge of the condition. Maybe I am wrong.

PR: No, no. Reading gives knowledge. Observation. Reading means what? Observing. *N'est-ce pas?* (Isn't it?) *Comme un livre.* (Like a book.)

Q: But knowledge in Sahaj Marg can only be like that?

PR: 'Like that' means like what?

Q: Sometimes when we want to find the right attitude with an abhyasi, it does not come, it comes like that. It does not come through reading.

PR: Who said that attitude comes from reading?

Q: No, no. But it comes through surrendering. So it is not knowledge which comes from the mind, but it comes from surrendering.

PR: Even when you have surrendered, you have to have knowledge. There are two possibilities: knowledge by study, knowledge by revelation. Knowledge by study is always our effort. Knowledge by revelation comes by the grace of the Master, when we surrender. And revelation is given only when we cannot study ourselves. When it exceeds our capacity, you see, not before. Otherwise it becomes a miracle and there are no miracles in Sahaj Marg.

Q: Are you sure there are no miracles? [laughter]

PR: I have not seen any.

Thursday, July 14, 1988

Q: What about Don?

PR: Well I saw the dawn, but I did not see the miracle. [he laughs] [laughter]

Q: The transformation of the self is a miracle.

PR: *Oui,* but you do not see miracles, you know. We think we are growing, we think we are making, doing, so many things. That is where the ego comes.

Q: The miracle is the opening of the heart.

Q: No, no. It is Him that makes the miracle.

Q: Yes! It is a miracle.

PR: The biggest miracle is that we are able to speak of miracles. No, no, you see, knowledge! Babuji had, I mean, total surrender to his Master, but he had to study. Have you not seen him study? And has he not told you several times, "I have to study your condition? And if I am not able to do it, I will refer it to Lalaji." Has he not said so many times? So, if it is necessary for Master, is it not necessary for you? Simple.

There was a young shepherd who was a whiz kid in mathematics, you know, a genius. And his father did not like him because he was too intelligent. One day there was a big flock of sheep. And this fellow always used to say, there are thirty-nine here, twenty-six there. And his father used to count, and it was always right. He was very angry. One day there was a huge flock of sheep. The father asked him, very scathingly, "Can you tell the number of sheep here?" The boy looked and said, "Oh, it is about seven hundred and forty-eight." [laughter] The father counted it and it was exact. He asked, "How did you do it?" The boy said, "I counted the number of legs and divided it by four." [uproarious laughter]

Bedbugs — do you know the bedbug? What do you call the bedbug? The bug in the bed. You know, so many medicines have been tried: insecticides, pesticides. One man came out with a novel medicine: one bottle costing only half a rupee. And he said, "Sure bug killer. Follow instructions for results." He sold a lot of bottles because in that village there were a lot of bugs. After one month he came around and everybody was waiting with sticks [he chuckles] [laughter] to meet him. They said, "We have not been able to kill a bug." He said, "Did you read the instructions?" They said, "What is there to read about killing a bug?" He said, "Aha! That is the problem, you see. You people do not read the instructions. I told you to read the instructions." He took out the paper. He said, "You see how beautifully I have planned it. Catch a bug. [he chuckles] [laughter] Put it on its back. Take a stick and gently press its neck. [laughter] When it opens its mouth put a drop of medicine in it. [laughter] [he laughs] Now try it." And he walked away. [laughter] [he laughs]

Q: Can you breathe here?

PR: Can we breathe?

Q: Yes. Or you don't need to breathe now any more? Is there still air here?

PR: A lot of it.

Q: We are living on pure prana now. [laughter] [he laughs]

PR: Well, without *prana* you would not exist.

Q: Yes, I feel it.

Q: So you become very effective if you can, in the short time, give a sitting that will give a long effect.

PR: That is what you do. In fact I can tell you, in this one week, you have received so much you would not have got in two years normally.

Q: Pressure cooker.

Thursday, July 14, 1988

Q: Babuji once told me, "I have given a little, but it will last long."

PR: Yes. It is the seed, you see.

Q: And are we able to, I mean, to receive it to that extent?

PR: Yes. It is like putting gas in a cylinder, compressing it and taking it. You know, ten thousand cubic feet of gas compressed into a cylinder under pressure and you can release it as you want, nothing wonderful. You know, the whole problem is the Western mind's tendency to compartmentalize. What it can do in one field, it will not try to do in another field. For instance — condition. You know, if a car is going in front of you and the exhaust is colored, you say the engine is not performing properly, or the fuel burner is not performing properly, or the carburetor. You can immediately diagnose. Isn't it? That is condition. Now, whether it is a 50cc engine or a 500cc engine has nothing to do with it. That is the power of the engine. Where it is located? It may be rear-mounted, front-mounted, it does not matter. It is still clumsy. This is condition. Why can't you use this knowledge in spirituality? Here you confuse position, condition, aura, I do not know what else. It is because, you see, this is my discovery now during the seminar, all of you have been confusing condition for approach, when the condition is good, approach is high. It has nothing to do with that.

Q: My experience is, that having lived for some years in different countries, that words are used differently.

PR: No, no. In Sahaj Marg we have only one set of words. Condition is always condition. You see, a patient may be dying, his condition may be good, subjectively. Another may be suffering a lot, but his illness may be relatively superficial. You can be psychosomatic and have pains which do not exist at all. Isn't it? The condition is there. But the inner state is different in each case.

Courmettes

Q: It is our linear thinking that makes us confuse things.

PR: Yes, exactly, you see.

Q: Is the feeling of this unity.

PR: Now? You all feel it. Yes.

Q: Yes?

PR: Yes. If you look inside you will feel.

Q: Is it a reflection of your condition?

PR: You cannot help it, you know. It is like all of you have the same food and you are all happy, and all a little somnolent and, you know, you close your eyes. Except for a man like Dario, who lights a cigar [laughter] and spoils the atmosphere instantly. [he chuckles] [laughter] You see? We share that condition, isn't it, at that moment. I mean, you cannot help not sharing it. And that brings you to another understanding, you see, that we really do not share. You see, sharing implies that I have something which I, sort of, partition out for everybody, you know, "Share this bread amongst all of you." So we cut it and share it. But when you share a condition, you share it because it is a common condition. There is no giving and taking, you see. So you see, sharing is used in a different sense. "We share an apartment." Are you cutting it into pieces? So you see, we have to understand this sharing is made possible because the Master gives the same condition to all. Direct sharing of the material wealth, where you have to fragment and share, you know. Therefore material wealth is always shared only by cutting into bits and distributing. So, every time you share it, the share gets lesser and lesser. Here the giver gives the condition at any level, and we do not have to lose, we always gain. So here, by sharing we gain; there by sharing we lose, in the material world. Now if you talk of sharing in spirituality, and you think of it in the material framework, you are afraid.

Thursday, July 14, 1988

Oh, how can I share my happiness? Will I not lose something? But here we only gain by sharing. You see how many, I mean, fascinating differences there are. And we can understand only when we experience. *S'il vous plait.* (If you please.)

Q: It is also experience which is confused in Europe, and therefore we do not know how to use the words.

PR: No, no, no.

Q: If we are talking about brain and soul and mind. We do not know the difference.

PR: No, but that does not matter. But when you talk of condition at least you should know. Semantically, there are so many differences, we do not bother. But this is a simple thing we all experience, we are all doing. And this we do not understand, because we do not apply one set of laws in one framework to the same in another framework. All universal laws are universal, not only because they apply everywhere, but because they apply to everything, you know, whether it is spirituality or materiality, or whatever it is. They must, otherwise they cannot be universal.

Yes. So we have to learn, no?

Q: Yeah, yeah.

PR: And there is also another, you know, Lotte, there is a difference in approach to learning. We learn by learning one thing. Western mind wants to learn by comparison. Therefore, you are always learning more things. "Buddha said this." "No, no, but the Moon says this, and the Dalai Lama says this." What are we worrying about Dalai Lama and Moon for? You stick to what you have to learn. When you study chemistry, do you say, "Oh, but in physics it says like this, and in geology it says like this?" You don't! Isn't it? You study physics. Otherwise, your professor raps you on the head. So here also, we must study one. And when we are perfect in it then, if it is necessary for your advancement, you may study other things. But it is never necessary, you see. If I am going in a lift, for instance, I do not have to know how the next lift is going. I am only worried whether this lift will take me to the top floor of the building. So this comparison does not apply. As Babuji said, I think, in connection with God, knowledge of God, "He cannot be known by comparison, because there is nothing to compare Him with." What will you compare Him with, and say, "God is like this." So comparison is of no use. Knowledge is absolute. Learn that which you have to learn. Do not compare it with another field or another system.

Q: I thought this was one of the definitions of the human being, that we were able to learn by abstract thought, by experience, by comparison, rather than just learning by experience.

PR: That is a Western formulation of knowledge. That is what I started out by telling you, like your logic, you know, from particular to generals and generals to particular. In the East, we believe logic is the law that governs the existence of something. It does not need comparison. It does not need contrast. It does not need to go from particular to general or general to particulars.

Q: In your speeches one can see this also, that you apply the principle of the thought you want to say, and then you shine a different aspect of the same. So it is a more circular thing. And we get confused by often forgetting this principle, because we go from A to B to C. So more causal thinking, and therefore we lose the oversight.

PR: Yes, but we must remember Babuji's famous statement that, "There can be causes without effects and effects without causes."

Thursday, July 14, 1988

Q: Yes, and therefore what you explained to us now is much more.

PR: Simple! Yes, I tell you, every talk I bring back to the origin. Now, this is nothing wonderful. Asimov wrote a series of books called the *Foundation Trilogy*, you know, *Foundation, Foundation and Empire, Second Foundation*. Then he wrote something else called *Foundation and Earth*. Then *Foundation's Edge*. Now his latest book is *Prelude to Foundation*, coming back to before *Foundation* started, which is a closing of the circle. If he does it, it is nice, he is a Westerner, a multimillionaire, book seller. Every book sells three million copies. He is right. But if an Oriental says, "Yeah, but, *aber*," you see, "*gibt's nicht so.*" (It cannot be like this.) Why? I have not seen anybody protesting about Asimov's *Prelude to Foundation*. "How come the beginning comes at the end?"

Q: I think the Eastern way is more the philosophical way of thinking, or principle way of thinking, and the Western is more a product oriented method.

PR: No, no, no, it is not like that. To the Western mind, what the Western mind does is right. For instance, you study all the philosophies, philosophical books written here — comparative religion. They do not deal with the East at all. Until, you know, Max Mueller came into the scene, some Vedic learnings came, and some concession to Buddhism, because it suits your idea of nihilism. You accept that which suits your temperament, not because it is good. It is a selective approach, even to knowledge, you see, "I will learn only that which suits my temperament." But knowledge is absolute. You must learn that which is right, not that which suits you. It is like an angry man who says, "I will look for that which promotes anger in me." So that catholicity of outlook, unless we are able to develop, you miss the truth. Truth cannot be what you say is the truth, or what I say is the truth. Truth is the truth, whether we accept it or not, whether we say it is the truth or not. It is immutable, absolute, ineffable. All these descriptions you give. But then, when you describe the truth in your books, you are always talking of Schopenhauer and Kant and all these fellows, you see. Why? Why is there no mention of people like Yagnyavalkya, for instance? Have you ever heard his name in the West? Perhaps no greater dialectician has ever lived.

Q: What was his name again?

PR: Yagnyavalkya. Or that little fellow Nachiketas, I told you his story. Who knows his name in the West? You see, you are all putting yourself into an intellectual cage just because you have been successful in the material side of life. And your success reflects in your standard of living, in your arrogance, in your pride, in your clothes, in your cosmetics, in your ability to help the undeveloped world by distributing your ill-gotten gains, all exploited wealth, you know. So you think your philosophy must also be supreme, your knowledge of God must also be supreme, your God must be the highest. Where is the real approach to knowledge? Therefore, we are tied up into knots. We have this, what they call 'the bind,' you know — the Americans. That way the Americans are better. For all their stupidity and arrogance, which you cannot beat, yet they have an open mind.

Q: But we get reward in thinking in this European way, and we are punished if we are thinking it.

PR: No, no, it is not punishment, Lotte. It is we who punish ourselves, you see.

Q: Yeah, yeah, in school and everywhere.

PR: No, no, but after you leave school, you can develop. You know, in school I was as stupid as you. Not that I am not so stupid still, but at least I have an open mind. I had difficulty

Thursday, July 14, 1988

accepting so many things from my Master, precisely because of my exposure to the West, you know. [he chuckles]

Q: Exposed?

PR: Yes, sunburnt! But you see here the potential, there so much potential. You have the ability, you have the accessibility, you have the capacity. More, you have the resources. You know, you are wasting enormous sums of money on education, educating in the wrong way. If you could divert it in the right way — all that you have to do is to open the doors of the mind. No?

Q: In Himalaya young abhyasis told us, "Here somebody thinks that all in the West is best."

PR: Yes.

Q: The trouble is that in the West they always trace everything back to Greek philosophy. That was the big thing. And, of course, it is very relatively lately.

PR: Yes, yes, for the last three years I have been telling you, you could read in my talks that, "The bane of European civilization is the Greek origin. They corrupted you thousands of years ago, and you have not got rid of it yet." Body consciousness, body beautiful, you know, two concepts which are totally detrimental to your morality and your philosophies, which you derived from the Greeks.

Q: Babuji said this also about the Greeks.

Q: It is not even that the Greek is right or wrong, it is always talked of as if that was the beginning.

PR: It is the *summun bonum*, you see, not only the beginning but the end.

Q: What about Socrates?

Courmettes

PR: He was also Greek. It is not a question of this belief or that belief. You see the effect it has on you? Wine is good, but the effect it has on you is drunkenness. Isn't it? So we do not drink. Wine by itself — what is wrong with wine? Such a nice color, beautiful red, you know, ruby red, claret red, whatever it is, keep it in the bottle and admire it. [laughter] Isn't it?

It is the same thing with knowledge, any knowledge which makes you corrupt, go wrong, you know. Like knowledge of criminality, how to break open a safe. I mean, it is a knowledge worth having, it has its own technology, its precision. You ask a safe breaker, he will tell you how beautifully it can be done. Some of them are geniuses at work. You know, even the police departments sometimes, when they are not able to operate their number locks, for some reason the number is misplaced, they get one of these gangsters from the London underground, you know. They take him there and say, "Look, you reveal this and we shoot you tomorrow." And he says, "Yes. When you want me, you call me and otherwise you put me in the can." They do. It is periodically done. So that knowledge is necessary, but if you misuse it, it is gone. As Babuji said, you know, it was right here in Orly airport we were waiting for a plane, next to a gleaming bar. We were next to the bar, you see, beautiful stainless steel, chromium, glass, and he said, "What is in all those bottles?" I said, "Alcoholic drinks." He said, "Wine?" Because he knew only wine. For him wine meant alcohol. I said, "Yes." Then he said, "Look, I am telling you, we must be like that bottle. It contains all the wine but it does not get drunk." So similarly, we must have the world within us but not get intoxicated with the world. We must have knowledge but not be intoxicated by our knowledge. Here there is an intoxication with knowledge, knowledge which is unproductive. You take Western philosophy, to my mind it is silly to call it

Thursday, July 14, 1988

philosophy. Philosophy must be a way of living, not just something abstract.

So, we have all these quite substantial differences in outlook. And then what happens? It definitely affects your practice, because you think like a Westerner and you are practising yoga and every time I say something, there is this, not misunderstanding, but inability to understand. Because you still continue to think like that. You know, suppose I am operating a machine, each maintenance manual must be observed. How does it work? What are its parts? "No, no, no, but I remember having operated something in Poland." "What did you operate?" "A tractor." "But this is not a tractor, this is a tooling machine." So that it is a machine does not make it similar to another machine. They are all machines. You know, it is like the system of the theory of — what do you call it in math — sets, set theory.

So we have got to be very specific. The human mind must develop two abilities: to pick out the similarities, first. What is similar in all these? And what is not similar, what we have to avoid. Otherwise, it is like the man who goes to the car park and says, "My car was green," and all the cars are green, and he does not know which is his car. It happened to an abhyasi once. He went underground in Munich for parking, he forgot the place where he parked, and he knew his car of course, but there were so many cars like his. Finally he had to telephone the police. And they located his car and brought it out, and I think he had to pay one hundred marks or one hundred and fifty marks, something. See, today it is difficult.

Q: There is so much unlearning to do.

PR: So much unlearning to do. Precisely! That is why Babuji also said of spirituality that, "It is not becoming, it is unbecoming, undoing, removing the grossness, the veils that are surrounding us." Becoming naked in that spiritual condition.

Q: That is exactly what I have experienced, in that week, apart from the personal experience. I think it was a good start, to establish a common knowledge.

PR: Yes.

Q: A common learning.

PR: Yes, that is what I am telling you. You know, this week, to me, has been of profound importance. I do not know how you all feel. Because, for me, I have an open mind, you know, I see, I hear criticism, and I know what is going on in your mind. I am able to better know you all than I ever knew you before, your understandings, your misunderstandings, your prejudices. Everything has come out in this week, and it is correct, you see. Now, it helps us to keep what is necessary, and to remove what is not necessary. So, more than anybody else, it has helped me, and I hope I shall be able to help you better because of that. This I did not want to reveal but... [laughter]

Q: You have let the cat out of the bag.

PR: Not exactly. I still have many cats in it, which you do not know about. [laughter] Or perhaps just kittens!

Q: Shouldn't we leave you?

PR: No, no, but, Ivor, it is of the essence of education, that the teacher learns while he teaches. And the student learns while they are being taught. Otherwise there is no advancement, you see. Our schools, especially in India, are filled with teachers who do not learn once they have become a teacher. So, they teach the same thing over and over again, class after class after class, you see, and their subject has left them twenty years behind. The poor student comes out of school twenty years

Thursday, July 14, 1988

behind the present state of knowledge. What can you do with that?

Q: In any real learning, everybody has to learn, I think.

PR: No, no, there is no question of real or false learning. It is learning *per se*, you see. Some of you will remember, last year I told you, you know, children worship their parents. Ivor, they are some sort of gods, you know — parents. But when the boy becomes eleven, twelve, or thirteen — the god that failed. Why? Precisely because he has come up to your level of understanding or education.

We should give up all conceptual frameworks. Freedom means that, you know. Like, physical freedom means breaking down of walls. Isn't it? Mental freedom means breaking down all the conceptual walls that we have. Walls with names, walls with nationalities, walls with systematizations — everything has to go. Then we are in that freedom, you see, where we intuitively judge or perceive the truth of it, rather than perceiving truth by reflection and mentation. That is why it is called direct perception. And for that you must have an open mind. Otherwise you will say, "Oh, it just cannot be."

Q: With an open heart.

PR: Well, whatever name you want to give it. What about 'un-being'. It could be a state of un-being too. You see, the difficulty is we feel safe within a framework. It is like I told you this morning, a man who was in jail, a lifer, he is let out. He has lost all contacts, no relationship, nothing, he prefers to go back to jail. He feels safe. At least there is somewhere to sleep in. So there comes a stage, if you lose your freedom for too long, freedom becomes frightening, freedom becomes threatening, freedom becomes unacceptable. And we have become like that. We have, sort of, occluded our minds in so many frameworks: existential frameworks, conceptual frameworks, you know, that we are afraid to break out and go out. It is like somebody who does not want to open his door at night and go out. He says, "Where will I go in the dark?" Well, the same place where you go in the daylight. The scenery has not changed. The land has not changed. Because you cannot see it, you are afraid. In the daytime you think you can see it, therefore you are not afraid. The things are still the same. So it is my understanding that darkness conceals and illumination reveals. It is also a conceptual system.

Q: I was thinking, earlier, when you mentioned this framework, and the sitting lasting much longer than the time. That is our conceptual framework?

PR: Yes, it is a framework, that things must take place during the sitting. But what is a sitting? To us a sitting is when something is occurring. If it is day long, the sitting is day long. If it is continuous, it is continuous. We are getting somewhere after all. No, that is very difficult. The difficulty is fear. And we have many stupid proverbs, you know, in English, which I used to admire. "A bird in hand is worth two in the bush." But it kills initiative. It kills enterprise. Isn't it? Many proverbs are like that.

Q: Often I am very un-proud of my heritage.

PR: Even that is wrong. Neither proud nor un-proud. You see, there are two reasons for heritages. Either we derive pride, you know, "I belong to the Stewarts," or the Tudors, or whatever it is, you see, when they were great. And then when we come out of a family which never had any roots anywhere, unknown, and you become great, you create a father and a grandfather for, you know, lending you greatness. You have some pictures painted of them, put on your walls. "Oh, my dad." Because then we like to derive greatness. You see, it is like a rich man, who buys all the library editions of the great books: *Harvard Great*

Thursday, July 14, 1988

Books, Britannica Great Books. Because, for him, now knowledge becomes a prop. He does not want just money and power, you see, he wants, also, to be known as a wise man.

Q: He does not have to read them, just have them.

PR: He does not have to read them. Well, there used to be a time when they just had the bindings without anything in them. [laughter] Hand-tooled leather. It is a great joke.

Q: A sad joke.

PR: So we always try, you see. But on one side, if you look at it, it is a worthwhile tendency. It only means you are seeking completion. But not in this artificial, self-deceiving sense, but in a real sense, you see, where everything gets rounded up, in a single enterprise, in a single achievement, where all is contained. But we seek to complete by achieving bits of each, and trying to put them together into a unity. It does not work. It is like, you know, the tricks that the cinema world plays. It shows you the face of one actress; the voice singing is somebody else's. If there is a, you know, one of these enticing scenes of the girl with her legs in the water, it is the legs of another girl. And you put these composites together, and look for such a woman. She does not exist! You know that famous remark which Richard Burton made about Elizabeth Taylor, "She has bowed legs, and they are too short." But yet, he thought her beautiful enough to give her a diamond worth four and one half million dollars.

Q: Married her two times.

PR: So, you do not find that perfection, you see.

Q: I feel that being married is experiencing something, too.

PR: Well, [he laughs] marriage is an experience [he chuckles] and subsequently there are many experiences. [he laughs] And to be fair to the ladies, it works both ways.

Q: Yes, yes, always. I think this subject is getting very risky. [laughter]

PR: [he laughs] You are right! No, no, but I was talking for them. Is Joy here anywhere?

Q: Yes.

PR: [he laughs] This is not spiritual talk! [laughter] We are now coming down and the plane is about to land. [laughter]

Q: I thought that to go into a dynamic of change, through the introspection, was good.

PR: You see, I will tell you one thing, we have a feeling of guilt, anything, you see. In the Christian tradition, you go and confess to your father priest. Now, if you really believed in it, there should be no more guilt after the confession. But they confess, again and again, the same thing. It shows there is no faith in the system, or the guilt is so strong they cannot believe that God can forgive them. And most important, they expect some tangible sign of forgivingness. As if God will come and say, "Yes, I have forgiven you." But perhaps, even if that happened, you would not believe; because how can God come before us? See, that gives you a hint, that guilt can only be eradicated by faith. Here, that belief is not necessary, because if the cleaning is successful, it goes. Even guilt is an impression, arising out of a thought or an action. So what is the difference between guilt, or horror, or something else produced by some thought and action? As grossness, it has no difference. So if the preceptor's work is correct, it should go like everything else goes.

Q: Is it also lack of confidence?

PR: Faith, not confidence. Confidence is lower level, you see. Good morning! [laughter]

11

Friday, July 15, 1988

Q: There seem to be so many things that we want.

PR: Oh, we want so many things when we start, music of the spheres!

Q: It is said that it is just for a short time, but it is not a short time. It continues.

PR: I remember there is a proverb in English, "Fortune favours the fools." [he laughs]

Q: I do not understand.

PR: I saw Babuji in my chair, and you know his characteristic gesture when something is over, [stretching back his joined hands above his head] [laughter] he did that. So I knew it is really over now. Most characteristic. I have not seen it for a long time.

Q: He used to say: they are full.

PR: All the sittings, because somehow they come out in a graded series and nothing should be missed, if possible. I know some people say, "Oh, you had twenty-one sittings and I attended seven of them, Chari. That is one third." It is not interest, that we calculate in percentage. We do miss something when we miss a sitting in a series like this, you see. Otherwise it is okay, you know. Once we were in Madras, and Babuji Maharaj had come home. My father used to work, and he left at half past six in the morning. We all went to see Babuji. Suddenly at seven o'clock he said, "All of you sit." We were about twenty-five, he said, "Sit five in each row, five lines. I am going to do something special." We sat. I was in the last row. He said, "For each line of five persons I will transmit for three minutes. When I say, 'That's all', they should move out and the whole set advance like that for three minutes, fifteen minutes in all." I was right at the end. Then when he finished, he called all of us back in, and he said, "Today I have given you something which it will take you three years to digest." And then he smiled, you see, and he said, "You know, when the Master is there, you should be there all the time with him, because even he does not know when he is going to give something, and what he is going to give." It is something very spontaneous — the need of the moment, shall we say. When my Dad came back in the evening, I reported this to him. He was furious. He went to Master and almost, you know, shouted at him, "How can you do such and such thing?" He said "*Ah han*, but that is why I say, you know, when the Master is there, twenty-four hours you should be with him. You have lost it today, but I will try to make up for you."

Q: The physical presence is absolutely necessary? I mean, as Master's work knows no limitation of space, if one is present with him, even if it is not at the same place. If your father was remembering him, the physical presence should not be necessary.

PR: Well, when he is there, you should be there, you know, it is also a sort of etiquette.

Q: What about the people working with the computers, transcribing your speeches, and that sort of thing.

PR: Because they are working for the Mission they get something always — volunteers, they get. They do not have to attend, in fact they are told not to attend sittings. That is why I have said, the easiest way of winning the Master's heart is to work, not meditation and all this, you know.

Q: And not to meditate, you said?

Friday, July 15, 1988

PR: Nothing is necessary if you are volunteer. That is how, I think, I got. Well, I am not a great meditator or anything like that, never was. But somehow, soon after I met him, I started doing the work without even asking him. All the work I did I took upon myself. It never occurred to me that I should ask anybody for permission.

Q: What you did, Master? What kind of work?

PR: Well, everything, I started making photographs of Master for sale, printing books in Madras. You know, I started in 1964, by 1966 I had virtually taken upon myself all the physical aspects of the Mission and centred them in Madras.

Q: In 1966.

PR: Yes. Even correspondence, except spiritual correspondence, which used to go to Babuji direct. In the beginning, all were happy. Because they thought, you know, they have found one of these animals to bear the burden, beast of burden. But, I think, after the 1973 Lalaji centenary, people started worrying, because, even from 1967, I was too close to Master for their liking. So that is the secret, you see, easiest way is work for him with your heart. You all remember Babuji has said that, "I am working for Nature," you see, this is his quotation. I am quoting him, "And anyone who works for me is also working for Nature."

Q: Chariji, when he used the term Nature, he often did, is that synonymous really with God?

PR: He used it in two senses: with a lowercase 'n' it meant this nature, with capital 'N' it meant [looking upwards]. Even now, I rely more on my work for him than my devotion for him. [he laughs] [laughter] I would not hazard on my devotion. [he laughs] [laughter]

Q: Isn't there a certain amount of devotion in the work as well?

Courmettes

PR: No.

Q: How come?

PR: Well, maybe it develops later. But it is the easiest way, you see. People try meditation, they do not do it very successfully. They try cleaning, they do not have time for it. They try constant remembrance, and, as I often quote this American boy, he said, "I practise constant remembrance several times a day." Then how on earth are you going to make the grade? So, it is the easiest, to work. That is why preceptors are in a privileged state. I hope you all appreciate it. [laughter] [he laughs]

Q: Did anybody tell you that, as the years are going by, you yourself, you are becoming more and more like Master?

PR: It is as they say, you know, it is a consummation devoutly to be wished. [he chuckles] And sometimes I am also frightened. [he laughs] It is always the case, you see. It is not real fear. It is the question of, you know, how to say it? You see, for instance, I tell you, even when I was the secretary of the Mission, especially after 1974, say even from 1972, from the time I started travelling with Babuji to Europe, I was doing virtually everything that I am doing now, there was not much difference, you see. But I was happy, because there was somebody I could, you know, he took the responsibility, you see. I could smoke, go around joking with the abhyasis, eat ice cream near a swimming pool, all sorts of funny things. He was always there, you see, and we were going round and round him like the planets round the sun.

And now, suddenly you are thrown upon yourself, you know, and the responsibility, total responsibility, falls upon you. And if I have to become more like him, it is worse [he laughs] [laughter] in a way, you know. But I think it is some unfortunately fortunate destiny. Because I was his disciple, I told you, some four, five thousand years ago when he was

Friday, July 15, 1988

Patanjali. Now this is something you can believe or reject, I mean both that he was Patanjali and I was his disciple. [laughter] [he laughs] But he himself told me, so I do not doubt it, you see. Also, what happened, we were travelling back from Europe in that 1972 trip, and we were sitting side by side. Both of us were smoking, and suddenly Babuji looked, you know, with a grave face and he said, "You know, I cannot find him."

And then he told me he had been trying to find Patanjali in the brighter world, because he wanted to refer some point of yoga to him for clarification. The brighter world is where the liberated souls go. He searched once, he did not find him, he searched a second time, still he did not find him, and third time, when he could not find him, he referred to Lalaji, "Master, I could not find him there." So Lalaji said, "His liberation has not been given yet. Look within yourself." [laughter] [he laughs] And then Babuji smiles and tells me in his most beatific way, "You know Patanjali is going to be liberated in this life." [laughter] [he laughs] He did not say Ram Chandra, but Patanjali. [he laughs]

Q: When did Patanjali live?

PR: Well it is approximately four thousand five hundred years ago. Then he told me, "You were my disciple in that life too, and Kasturi was either your mother or your sister." So that shows, you know, how close we have been, and how this funny thing keeps intertwining and like this reverse shuttle and loom, 'trang, trang,' it goes up and down. Then he told me I had been his disciple in yet another life, but he said, "That is not important. It is no more necessary for you to know these things." He thought I would be happy. Really I was shocked. [laughter] I was really upset, you know. Here is the old man who claims to be Patanjali, and he is not liberated, [laughter] [he laughs] and worse, I was his disciple and I am still not liberated. [laughter]

So I was really shocked. I told Babuji, "What is this nonsense? You are still here, okay. [he chuckles] But me? What about me?" He said, "By Lalaji's grace, this will be your last life, too." And now, you know, Patanjali is held in the highest position in yoga in India — no Lalaji, no Ram Chandra, nobody. So I asked him, "How come you were not liberated in that life?" He said, "The way had not been opened, you see. Lalaji had to come and discover the method which could easily liberate." And for me the proof was that, though neither of us have studied Sanskrit, he was quoting Patanjali, 'Chapter eight, four' and you know, 'six, three' as if he had studied it. And even more surprising, I seem to understand Sanskrit, you know, in a sort of automatic way. And before I came to Babuji, I have done three or four years of yoga, hatha yoga and things like that, on my own. So it all ties up somewhere, here and there.

Q: Were any of us followers of Patanjali in our past lives?

Q: Yes!

PR: Well, I believe we must all have been connected with Babuji in one life or the other. That is why many come and go away who have not had the past connection, you see. It requires several lives.

Q: Chariji, could it be that Patanjali was not liberated because of the need that he would come?

PR: No, no, no, he can come even after he is liberated. Lalaji was never born before.

Q: How come, if we had been Patanjali's followers or in some connections, that we were born in the West?

PR: Well, some tendency drags you, you know. You see, there are many Indians who are living in India today, with clearly European tendencies. And there are many Europeans with an absolutely Indian way of living and life, attracted to India all

Friday, July 15, 1988

the time. They both have, you know, had the tendency, you see, the pull from the other direction and they are born there. Some tendencies of the past remain. That is why sometimes when I am strict and disciplined, you know, I think I must have been a German some time, [laughter] [he laughs] a real German, not a Bogota. [laughter]

Q: So you and Babuji have had a number of lives in between, is it?

PR: I know definitely we have had three lives together.

Q: With Babuji?

PR: Oh! Several lives in between of course.

Q: Master was not Kabir by any chance? He used to talk about him.

PR: No, no.

Q: You were talking about memory. Is this the real memory?

PR: Which?

Q: The memory of past lives you were referring to.

PR: Yes, I have felt, you know, for instance, even when I was a boy studying in Benares, when I first went to U.P., I felt at home. And every time I go to U.P. even now, you know, I feel some sort of a thrill. It is not external. It is something which shakes your heart, you see. That is the effect of the environment of the past. Several things: my fluency in Hindi without ever learning the language, finding a guru there. I mean, we have hundreds of thousands of gurus in India. How did I gravitate to this old man? That is why we must believe that we are called, you know. And, as Babuji once said, he can never cut the connection from us except under the most, perhaps what you can call, sinful conditions. And his definition of the greatest sin was ingratitude, not petty things like adultery and drunkenness and all these things — **ingratitude**. So why did I begin this? [laughter] I dropped somewhere.

Q: Chariji, you were making connections of lives and why.

Q: Yes, because the question was that you were looking more and more like Babuji.

Q: Master, what about Lalaji?

PR: He came once and that is all, you see. He came for a purpose.

Q: Where does he fit into the picture in between Patanjali and all this?

PR: Well, probably he came to wake up my old man and say, "Look what you have been and what you are doing still here, come on!" [he chuckles] I like to believe that he came to wake up this person who was asleep, similar to John the Baptist's baptism of Christ. No disrespect for Lalaji, because he did a very vital thing, you see.

Q: Coming from where?

PR: Coming from where? Coming from **there**. [he chuckles] [laughter] That is where we are all going, when you get there you will find out. [laughter]

Q: Chariji, is it true that when we all go back into the Centre, and the Centre contracts, we will all be blown out again?

PR: No, no, no. Nonsense. That is some sort of juvenile fear expressed by some people, you see, who still conceive of this universe in time and space. And one boy asked me, you see, "What happens at *pralaya*? You are drawn back into the source?" I said, "Yes." And he said, "When the next creation comes, will we come again?" I said, "Why are you bothered about it?" "No, no, but if I am going to come even after *pralaya*, what is the fun in doing all this?"

Friday, July 15, 1988

I discovered a very significant thing only very recently. You know, I have been studying this subject for, I do not know, nearly fifty years. Studying in a real sense, buying books, reading and analyzing, and co-referring this from that, from that to this, without a knowledge of Sanskrit. And everywhere I found that at the *mahapralaya* everything is dissolved into the Ultimate, you know. But I was very impressed recently, you know, just about a year back, when I read that there are these seven rishis. Now you see, this *dippa*, there are supposed to be those seven rishis in the Indian mythology; they continue through, even through that period. Because they are the ultimate controllers of everything. And it is significant that when Ramakrishna Paramahamsa was looking for his successor, you know, it is said that one of these rishis, you see, he seemed to topple, he did not fall, but some essence of his fell, and that was Vivekananda, his disciple. So they are the truly eternal entities. But you know, when you consider that whole cycle of four *yugas* and the night and the morning and all that sort of thing, it lasts something like, I do not know, four hundred and thirty-three billion years or something like that. It does not make sense to worry about what is going to happen after that. [he chuckles]

Q: But Babuji sometimes said that he worked on the next universe.

PR: Yes, there has to be somebody to do it, you know, that is what I am just telling you, the seven rishis. Who knows, perhaps he is one of them.

Q: I did not hear the question.

PR: Babuji said he is working for the next creation. But the next creation could be one of these smaller cycles of *pralaya*, you know. We have these four *yugas* and at the end of each *yuga* there is a *pralaya*. That is why the fourth *pralaya* is called the *Maha Pralaya*. And of course, he used to call our own dissolution, in the spiritual way, an individual *pralaya*. So, if you understand it correctly, *pralaya* really means a dissolution from which you do not return, you see. It is not an annihilation, it is becoming merged with the source. I did not know this, to answer that boy then.

Q: So *pralaya* is only the dissolution of the physical universe.

PR: No, no, of the self in all ways, you see. That is, you cease to exist as yourself, but you do not cease to exist in an absolute sense. In the ultimate sense, if you understand it, it is only a transformation. That is why I prefer to think of even evolution as a transformation, you see. And that is what I tried to suggest in one of my talks in Vorauf, you remember. That the Western idea of evolution as some sort of a qualitative growth is not valid. Because the essence is always the same. It only achieves different forms, in which it is possible to realise more and more of its essential nature, and that culmination comes in the human existence, you see.

Q: How did you say it, "It only achieves different forms."

PR: It is only assuming different forms in different existences in which it can progressively realise more and more of its essential nature. And when we come to the human condition, it is now the final realisation, as we call it. Therefore, we call it realisation, Self-realisation, God-realisation — not achieving, not getting, not even becoming. And it is significant that Babuji said, "Not becoming, but unbecoming," you see. And it is linked to consciousness, and without consciousness you cannot possibly realise. And after this realisation comes, you are now divine, in which ever state you are, you see. And if, with that realisation, you take the jump into the Infinite, it is over, you see, realisation leads to the merger with the Infinite at that single moment. Therefore Babuji said, "Turn your head

Friday, July 15, 1988

from here to here, and that is all that is necessary." It is possible in one instant of time.

Q: Don't we have a problem of space all the time? If we did not have this thinking of space we would not get so confused.

PR: We have this concept, you know, that space and time are interdependent, yes. But the eternity is beyond both. You see, there is this limited idea of eternity as endless time. Like you say, "And they lived forever after." You start with, "once upon a time," in the dim past and, "live ever after," in the dim future, and this we consider to be eternal. But eternity is something which transcends time.

Q: Did Babuji ever say whether there were other forms of lives in other worlds?

PR: Inevitably! Well, it is one of the peculiarly egocentric qualities of the human that he thinks he is the only thing created on earth. There must be forms of life everywhere. Nevertheless, this is the highest in the whole universe. Because Babuji has explained in *Reality at Dawn* — I do not know how you people can read *Reality at Dawn* and still ask these questions — because he sees the Ultimate as a sort of an egg-shaped thing, and there are many minor eggs which form the universe. But ours is the only egg connected directly with That. Therefore, from the human situation it is possible to go directly there — from no other place in the universe. So, even assuming there are forms of life everywhere else in the universe, one has to assume they will come here eventually as a human being before they can evolve to the final goal, you see. And it is significant that in yoga literature this world is called, 'the world of liberation.' Final journey can be taken off only from here. And as I quoted from the Gita, even Brahma, Vishnu, Shiva have to come down here and find their way up.

Q: So Lalaji could only have come here?

Courmettes

PR: Well, where else would he go?

Q: Anywhere.

PR: There are lesser liberated souls who can do the work in other worlds. It does not end with liberation. [he laughs] Do not have an idea of going on a holiday. [he laughs] [laughter] Liberated souls are throughout the universe, everywhere, controlling, regulating.

Q: Endless.

PR: No end to work! That is why I hope I reach the goal direct. [he laughs] [laughter] I do not want to be a traffic policeman on Venus or some such place [laughter] for the next ten thousand years. It is not likely but...

Q: Is it true that liberated souls, who have not realised the full journey, that they used to sit with Master in his little office?

PR: Liberated souls and non-liberated good souls who are in the limbo, you know, between births; they also come. They come seeking, you know, some solace, some consideration from the Master. Once Babuji said, "Today, you know, there were two souls present here." So I said, "No, Master, we were seventeen today." [laughter] He said, "No, no, I meant souls, S-O-U-L, you know, soul." I said, "What were they doing here?" Then he said, "You know, halfway through the meditation I saw them coming through the window, and they were quietly sitting there praying for my help. Do you want to see them?" [laughter] [he laughs] I said, "No." Then he said, "There is nothing to be afraid of, they are good souls." And then he said, "They come wherever there is meditation. You will always find one or two hanging around." I said, "If you tell this to abhyasis, they will not come for satsangh." [he laughs] [laughter]

Friday, July 15, 1988

Q: I thought that once you had said that once we die, and we are not liberated, we lose consciousness.

PR: Not at all. If you are of that level, you know, which was almost liberated, but not quite liberated; the good souls continue for a very long time, sometimes thousands of years. And you know, you cannot really say, is it consciousness or is it just attraction, like a magnet attracting inconscient matter, like iron filings? But liberated souls, for instance, carry their consciousness with them. It is given to them. Yes it is possible to have consciousness. You see, in the yogic tradition even rocks have a consciousness, but it is almost totally inactive, like zero Kelvin or whatever it is, temperature, you know.

Q: Absolute zero.

PR: Absolute zero. They are almost totally unconscious, but the faculty of consciousness is dormant. It cannot go anywhere you see. You remember I told you when the person dies there is an immediate recapitulation and the decision where to be born, how to be born. How can we take it without consciousness? But they cannot use that consciousness except for a limited purpose. For instance, a soul which has not been liberated cannot use the consciousness to go further, it has to come back here. But it has a limited function in examining and coming to a judgement: what should I be? Where should I be? How should I be?

Q: Master, so they still can pray?

PR: Yes, it is obvious that these souls can pray, they are higher souls that are nearly liberated.

Q: Can they still serve?

PR: Serve what? Work has to be given. There is no such thing as service, you see. That is why our certificate says 'permitted', not 'qualified', you see. That is why, in the Eastern wisdom, there is not much respect for qualification. Because when you are permitted to do something, you get the ability to do something, side by side. When he gives the work, he gives the power to do it. And when you ask for power, it is crazy, you know, because all the power in the world that you need for that work, you get. When it is finished, you are again powerless. In that sense, it is only a man who is working continuously for Him who retains the powers, and gets more and more as he needs, you see. What would we do with power without work? It is power grossness.

Q: Why is this forty days after death mentioned in most traditions?

PR: I do not know. In all traditions it is there, forty or forty-one, forty-four, something like that. In all traditions.

Q: They say that the soul hangs around for forty days.

PR: Before it goes.

Q: Because of the pain?

PR: But I do not think it is really correct. It may be in some sort of, I do not know, religious way. But according to Sahaj Marg, the really bad soul, you know, I mean in the sense — there is no bad soul — really samskara-burdened soul takes almost immediate birth. But the good soul waits because he has to find the environment suitable for his evolution. And it is not easy to find nowadays.

Q: It seems like, something like, density or grossness, the less it is, the higher and lighter you are.

PR: Yes. And the longer we wait.

Q: The soul then waits hundreds of years before being born.

PR: Thousands of years. It depends, you know. In the old days, when there was a more congenial atmosphere for spiritual growth, I suppose even good souls could be born at once and

Friday, July 15, 1988

save time. But now they have to hang around. Now here is a very funny invertendo, you know, the grosser souls get the immediate chance to be born at least, you know, and then you can make your way. So that is why we should try to leap out of this into that and not, you know, stay in between. You understand?

Q: Do you remember, I think it was in Denmark, talking about birth control, and Master laughed and then he whispered to you I think it was, I do not remember what it was.

PR: Somebody was talking about population control. He said, "Really speaking, I am the only person who is doing it. Because a soul I liberate never comes back." [laughter] And it is true, you know. They are gone once and for all. No more circling about here.

Q: So abhyasis should have many children?

PR: It does not mean that at all. It only means anyone should be able to get his grace. Why only abhyasis? I do not see why. We were not abhyasis' children. Not you, not me.

Q: You once said that a child that is born...

PR: Yes, preferably; but then you must be evolved enough for your child to benefit. Very often I find children are very good and the parents are withdrawing from their status. [he chuckles] You see, there is a mission called the Radha Swami Satsang in India. And there, there was a man who's father was a master and who's son was a master of that tradition, you see. He did not find the way in between. He is famous in their history as the father of a master and the son of a master. It is not enough. What you are, you see, is all that matters. And it holds, you know, the son of a millionaire is not necessarily a rich man, he may squander, he may get sick, he may gamble.

Q: The use of contraception must be very frustrating to souls, isn't it?

PR: At the higher levels, yes. I mean, at the higher level of human beings. At the lower level it does not matter because there are innumerable millions of them. Not of importance.

Q: And cannot Master liberate the soul when it is nearly liberated?

PR: It can be done if there is a master who is willing to do it. You have one example of Vivekananda having done it when he was in the U.S. He was walking on the seashore and he was approached by a soul which was desolate, and it is said that he liberated that soul. For the Master nothing is impossible. I suppose he could even liberate us before our birth, I do not know.

Q: You have work to do.

PR: But, you see, that soul must have at least the ability to attract the Master's attention.

Q: Those souls who are coming to meditate with Master in the presence of Master?

PR: Perhaps he liberated some of them, I do not know. I know that on the 14th of August every year he liberates one soul in memory of his Master. Pujya Lalaji's *mahasamadhi* day.

Q: But if we came from the source, why is all this trouble and suffering to go back to the source?

PR: Read the literature. [laughter] It is all given there. You see, the simple example: we have in gaseous form water vapour — it is free; it is mobile; it can move anywhere; it cannot be contained; it can expand or contract at will. It falls as rain — it is already limited by its form; it can still be mobile, but not as it was. And when you condense it further it becomes ice — it is solid, immovable, heavy, everything, you see. The thing is

Friday, July 15, 1988

the same. This is gross, that is subtle. So Babuji used to say, "The human being is gross, God is the subtlest." Therefore, as we drop our grossness by cleaning, by change of our ways of life, we become subtler and subtler and approach the divine state. So again, you come to that point, which I was saying, there is no evolution as such. Only thing, you are giving up the grossness.